Leveraging Library Resources in a World of Fiscal Restraint and Institutional Change

Given the continuing cataclysmic shift in the economic landscape in the last few years, librarians have been forced to reevaluate not only the traditional services that they offer but also their continued existence and relevance to their academic institutions. Given the 'new normal' of tighter constraint on personnel and materials budgets, librarians now are compelled to find new ways of offering services and forging new relationships with departments and programs outside the traditional library setting.

This volume highlights a number of projects being implemented in academic libraries including: rethinking the entire concept of a library, redefining physical space for new collaborative uses, adapting entrepreneurial techniques to acquire funding, creating new research tools and improving services, forging new consortial partnerships, allying more closely the mission of the library with that of the institution, and adapting public library programs to academic libraries. By re-examining the purpose of an academic library under continuing financial duress, librarians can ensure that their libraries will continue to have relevance to higher education.

This book was published as a special issue of *College & Undergraduate Libraries*.

Kevin B. Gunn is Coordinator of Religious Studies and Humanities Services at The Catholic University of America Libraries in Washington, DC.

Elizabeth Dankert Hammond is Dean of University Libraries, Mercer University. A graduate of the University of Illinois, Ms. Hammond joined Mercer in 1978. Her professional activities include service with ACRL and on the Boards of SOLINET and LYRASIS.

Leveraging Library Resources in a World of Fiscal Restraint and Institutional Change

Edited by
Kevin B. Gunn and
Elizabeth Dankert Hammond

Routledge
Taylor & Francis Group
LONDON AND NEW YORK

First published 2013
by Routledge
2 Park Square, Milton Park, Abingdon, Oxon, OX14 4RN

Simultaneously published in the USA and Canada
by Routledge
711 Third Avenue, New York, NY 10017

First issued in paperback 2017

Routledge is an imprint of the Taylor & Francis Group, an informa business

This book is a reproduction of *College and Undergraduate Libraries*, vol. 18, issue 2-3. The Publisher requests to those authors who may be citing this book to state, also, the bibliographical details of the special issue on which the book was based.

British Library Cataloguing in Publication Data
A catalogue record for this book is available from the British Library

Typeset in Garamond
by Taylor & Francis Books

Publisher's Note
The publisher would like to make readers aware that the chapters in this book may be referred to as articles as they are identical to the articles published in the special issue. The publisher accepts responsibility for any inconsistencies that may have arisen in the course of preparing this volume for print.

ISBN 13: 978-1-138-10924-7 (pbk)
ISBN 13: 978-0-415-53875-6 (hbk)

Contents

Introduction

In the last three years, we have seen the economic landscape shift under academic libraries. Librarians have had to reposition themselves in creatively managing their institution's library resources. With little new money, fewer staff being hired or replaced, and materials budgets frozen or cut, librarians have been forced to take stock of their situation. With funds tighter than usual, a different type of fiscal restraint has entered the halls of academe. Leveraging library resources has become the 'New Normal' for many of us. Some of the themes of this shift include re-engineering the library, creating new tools and services, making new consortial arrangements, and meeting institutional priorities.

Theoretical

Our opening section has two articles that question the existence of the traditional library. In **New Wine, New Wineskins**, McDonald proposes an Information and Learning Center (ILC) to replace the traditional academic library. The ILC would overcome the limitations of traditional roles of academic librarians in such areas as library instruction and collection development by shifting the focus onto a new type of position, the information and learning specialist, who would be available to focus exclusively on the individual student's needs rather than on the needs of the academic library. **Other People's Money: Adapting Entrepreneurial Techniques to Build Capital in Challenging Economic Times** by Farrell discusses the "predator" model of entrepreneurship as an alternative to the "collaborative imperative" of traditional information literacy models.

Case Studies

Smith and Galbraith, in **Library Staff Development: How Book Clubs Can Be More Effective (and Less Expensive) than Traditional Trainings,** argue for the inexpensive implementation of employee book clubs to foster professional development. In **The NYU Survey Service: Promoting Value in Undergraduate Education**, Phillips, Guss, and McGarry discuss the establishment of a Web survey tool by the Data Service Studio to allow university affiliates to create and administer surveys for their own ends.

In **Engaging the Campus Community through New Roles and New Relationships: The McMaster University Library Postdoctoral Fellowship Program**, Trzeciak, MacLachlan, and Shenker write of funding three postdoctoral scholars through fellowships from the Council of Library and Information Resources to facilitate the creation of the Virtual Museum of the Holocaust and the Resistance, the opening of the Lyons New Media Centre, and new teaching opportunities at McMaster University in Hamilton, Ontario, Canada.

Collaboration With Other Units on Campus

In **Cool Collaborations: Designing a Better Library Experience,** Fox, Carpenter, and Doshi demonstrate a number of projects in the library at the Georgia Institute of Technology, including a 'virtual' aquarium, 'virtual' posters to showcase students' research, an exam relief program called "Stress-Buzzters," a library rock 'n roll radio show, and last, a display wall for architecture students, all highlighting the opportunities of doing interesting projects with minimal funds. **The Third Place: The Library as Collaborative and Community Space in a Time of Fiscal Restraint** by Montgomery and Miller addresses the concept of space and how libraries must reinvent themselves as spaces for collaborative learning and community interaction in order to be considered the third place after work and home. In **Strategically Leveraging Learning Space to Create Partnership Opportunities,** Doan and Kirkwood discuss the new LearnLab in the Management & Economics Library at Purdue University. This new type of space created within the traditional library has encouraged unique and unexpected opportunities for collaboration with other university programs and initiatives within the institution's strategic plan. Lastly, **Hitching Your Wagon to the Right Star: A Case Study in Collaboration** by Engle describes her adventures in establishing a library presence in the first-year orientation program at Texas A & M University, commonly known as 'Fish Camp.'

Collaboration With Other Libraries

In **Delivering Information Literacy Instruction for a Joint International Program: An Innovative Collaboration Between Two Libraries,** Alleyne and Rodrigues discuss a collaborative project between Mount Saint Vincent University Library in Halifax, Nova Scotia, Canada and Bermuda College Library in Hamilton, Bermuda. Their paper demonstrates how international cooperation between institutions can occur for classes in library instruction and information literacy. Wagner and Gerber discuss the implementation and sharing of a Digital Asset Management System (DAMS) among the eight institutions that make up the Cooperating Libraries in Consortium (CLIC) in Saint Paul and Minneapolis, Minnesota. **Building a Shared Digital Collection: The Experience of the Cooperating Libraries in Consortium** outlines the selection, acquisition, implementation, maintenance, and ongoing assessment of the system.

Kevin B. Gunn, MA, MLIS
Elizabeth D. Hammond, MLS

New Wine, New Wineskins

JOSEPH McDONALD
Malone University, Canton, Ohio, USA

Academic libraries face an uncertain future. Rather than attempting to develop libraries based on an unknowable future, the author argues it is preferable to address student learning needs with a set of information and learning instructional services established on teaching and learning principles and activities. Evolving from and replacing the present academic library, this new organization, the information and learning center, is staffed by a new academic professional, the information and learning specialist, who addresses the student's need to gather and manage information, read, and write as an integrated set of experiences directed by the curriculum and teachers' pedagogies.

> Only the action that is moved by love for the good at hand has the hope of being responsible and generous. Desire for the future produces words that cannot be stood by. But love makes language exact, because one loves only what one knows. One cannot love the future or anything in it, for nothing is known there. And one cannot unselfishly make a future for someone else. Love for the future is self-love—love for the present self, projected and magnified into the future, and it is an irremediable loneliness. (Berry 2005, 61)

The future of academic libraries, never far from professional concerns, is now engaging librarian thought and speculation with what seems an unusual intensity and urgency. In 2010, the Association of College and Research Libraries (Staley and Malefant 2010) presented twenty-four scenarios for the possible state and condition of academic libraries in the next fifteen to twenty years. These addressed many possible futures based on an equally daunting set of assumptions. A discussion of them and the process by which the assumptions and scenarios were derived is beyond the scope of this article. Nevertheless, a brief description of the ones understood to be the most likely to occur seems useful and will be a foil against which an alternative understanding of the library's future can be presented.

Nine scenarios were seen as those with a high probability of occurring and having a high impact on libraries:

1. Breaking the textbook monopoly
   Teachers will create their own course materials and will not rely on external publishers.
2. Bridging the scholar/practitioner divide
   Librarians will become the mediators of the large amount of material made available as scholars and practitioners engage in timely dialogue, making scholarly materials more quickly available than by the normal peer review process.
3. Everyone is a "nontraditional" student
   "Students are active in designing their own learning outcomes, and the personalized curriculum becomes the norm" (Staley and Malefant 2010, 12).
4. I see what you see
   Large touch screen tables placed beneath cameras and projectors in computing labs and libraries change the way group designing is conducted.
5. Increasing threat of cyberwar, cybercrime, and cyberterrorism
   Seen in challenges to the privacy of information versus institutional and national security.
6. Meet the new freshman class
   Involves dealing with the information technology divide among students who are "information" fluent and those who are not.
7. Right here with me
   Technology will allow students to scan information "on the fly" and work with learning group members, anywhere.
8. Scholarship stultifies
   Scholarly publishing will change dramatically, but "collegial culture continues to value tradition over anything perceived as risky" (Staley and Malefant 2010, 18).
9. This class brought to you by . . .
   The rise of for-profit institutions and the disaggregation of learning.

In four of these scenarios, the speed of change was thought to be especially fast:

- Increasing threat of cyberwar, cybercrime, and cyberterroism
- Meet the new freshman class
- Right here with me
- Scholarship stultifies

Because, according to the scenario builders, these fast changing scenarios are also highly likely to occur, libraries are urged to begin planning now to act on them. To make these scenarios "actionable," Staley and Malefant urge library leaders to ask four questions:

- Do we have the resources to take advantage of this scenario, if it were to exist today?
- In what ways are we unprepared to deal with this scenario?
- If we had all the resources we needed, how could we leverage this scenario to our advantage?
- What would need to happen in the internal and external environments for the previous scenario to become real?

Two immediate observations can be made about these scenarios. One, they are heavily oriented toward technology and its implications for the library rather than providing insight into student learning. Two, although none of these scenarios concerns trivial matters, none of them goes to the core reasons why a student attends college.

In addition to the ACRL documents, a sampling of the literature in the past five years on topics related to the future of the academic library revealed much of this heightened concern for various aspects of the profession's future, here and abroad. Much of this concern for the future of libraries expressed in the literature is largely premised on the conviction that unless one understands or can reasonably picture what lies in the future, it is difficult, if not impossible, to prepare properly for that future.

This article takes a different approach and argues that it is better to design a desirable or preferred present, based on the missions and objectives of existing institutions of higher education, than to attempt to design for an imaginary or hypothetical future and one that may never materialize in the ways predicted, if at all. We cannot know what will be "valued" in the future. We only know what is valued in the present. It seems counterproductive to have what we do in the present determined or conditioned by what we do not know will happen in the future.

Most of the scenarios and predictions in the literature rely on the sometimes heavy presence of information technology and its possible or likely impact on libraries and their services. To put it in its simplest form, the computer is always present, active, shaping, or determining library futures. It is regarded almost as a force of nature, always to be reckoned with, always indispensable. What the library may or may not do or become in the future, it seems, is always subordinate to the omnipotent presence of information technology.

In this article, I do not critique the present or expected role of computers in libraries. Needless to say, it is highly likely they will be, if not a force of nature, at least a continuing and enlarging force of technology at the intersection of academia and organized formal knowledge. However, a heavy focus on technology tends to do two things. One, it reduces our interest in what libraries might accomplish to that which can be realized only with technology. It puts limits on our imagination of what is possible or desirable. If it is not digital or streaming or expressed in pixels or discussed in terms of networks or large screens, or conversely small screens and devices, we prefer to give it second place in our thinking, or not think about it at all. Two, whatever we might imagine libraries doing, even matters such as reference service or information literacy instruction tend to be seen, frequently uncritically, through the lenses of technology, to the exclusion of other perspectives. Privileging technology makes some things possible. It also limits or eliminates other pursuits that may be equally or more desirable.

The central thesis of this article is that rather than attempting to develop a future for college and undergraduate libraries on a foundation of information technology, the teachers and especially the learners in the institutions sponsoring these libraries are best served by information organizations that are designed and developed on a foundation of service for student learning needs and student learning success, derived from the core values of the curriculum and the professional and academic commitments of teachers. "Library" and information literacy and technology serve a secondary, supporting, not necessarily unimportant, role.

Furthermore, as librarian focus changes from technology and the "collection" to the learning needs of students and the teaching requirements of their instructors (not as "information literacy"), how libraries conduct business will change. In responding to these changes, an organization will evolve, by design, bearing little resemblance to the present academic library organization. And, as I will show below, in creating services and activities at the information and learning nexus, which enfold the curriculum and teachers as their central and determining elements, a different kind of information professional may evolve, one fully engaged with student learning, broadly and at many levels, one quite different from today's model of the academic librarian.

WHY TEACHING AND LEARNING?

What, after all, is inappropriate with information and its technologies as the foundations for academic libraries? The simple answer is that these are not at the heart of student learning, which is the core purpose, the essential mission of a college.

However, librarians have maintained for decades that the library is the heart, the core of the college. Librarians are informed by a different vision, a different set of professional ethos than that which informs and animates the rest of the college. Historically, and by virtue of professional preparation, librarians owe their allegiance to the "collection," to its enabling and supporting technology, and to activities that inform users or allow them to discover what is available in the collection, which presumably has some relevance to students' needs for formal knowledge content in learning or to teachers for teaching or guiding learning. For librarians, in the conduct of their professional obligations, information trumps teaching and learning. For the institution, its curriculum, teachers, and students, teaching and learning are much more important than information. For the librarian, information informs learning ("information literacy"); for the teacher and student, learning informs information ("literate information").

The content of libraries, "information," has always been close to the professional efforts of teachers. Libraries, after all, hold much of the material, the documents, the formal substance of what is to be taught and what the teacher expects the student to learn. But librarians will need to be connected to teaching and learning, though teaching and learning presently lie outside the professional interests and preparation of librarians; as Bennett observed, "It is regrettable that library claims to support learning and teaching are so rarely backed by any formal, systematic understanding of these most fundamental activities of higher education" (2003, 22). He further noted, "In considering how library space might best facilitate student learning and faculty teaching, topics not squarely within librarians' professional competence in the way that library operations are, the evidence is clear that librarians rarely undertake systematic assessments or seek substantive guidance from students and faculty themselves" (35).

WHAT ARE TEACHING AND LEARNING?

Teaching, at its simplest, is the intentional act of creating the conditions and circumstances for learning. Learning is considerably more than the accumulation of information. It is personal and intellectual development. Learners construct models of reality, and good teachers ask how this construction occurs and how it can be improved. Good learning aims at comprehension and the use of that understanding in reasoning, and learners are changed in ways that affect their hearts and minds and their ability to continue to grow.

How are teaching and learning connected to the library? How might they shape what a library is and does—other than providing "learning support?" And, why should they, rather than information and its technologies, be the foundation for the academic library?

I have already mentioned one reason why teaching and learning should form the foundation for the library. Students come to college to learn, not to find and use information or to use information technology. Information and its technologies are subordinate to the acts of teaching and learning, and the library's shape and structure should, accordingly, be determined by teaching and learning, the most important activities on campus and those to which the institution commits the largest part of its financial resources.

A second and related reason for making teaching and learning the foundation for academic library services lies in what is justice for the student. I define justice here as giving students what they deserve and need. The significance and importance of information lie largely in what is done with it, not in its mere discovery and organization. Many students have little idea of what do with information once they have it. Increasingly, they do not know how to read it, write about it, or enumerate with it. However, the library tells the student, in effect, well, that's too bad. The writing center is over there, the reading clinic is across the campus, the math lab is next door, and your teacher should have prepared you for this assignment, in any event. This is not treating the student justly.

Finding information requires prior insight so as to recognize when appropriate information is found. Context and meaning are more important than mere information and much more important than skill with the machine and systems used to find it. But in privileging information and technology the library sends the message that search and discovery rather than insight and application are the most important, that in finding and accumulating information the student has successfully accomplished learning and intellectual development.

Another aspect of justice for the student as something they deserve is the increasingly heavy use of adjunct faculty. Students deserve good teachers committed to successful student learning. Although there are adjunct faculty who go beyond their contract to simply meet a class and cover the material in the syllabus, many do not and are not expected to do so. Students, increasingly more of them, are usually shortchanged or dealt with unjustly. I am convinced that a library, with a foundation in teaching and learning, well connected to the classroom, can do much to help students in such situations, which are becoming much more common, as well as in those situations where a student taking an online course needs more learning support than that made available through e-mail, a threaded discussion, a chat facility, FAQs, and so forth.

At this point, some may object and say that collecting and providing access to information and teaching students how to find and manipulate this information and its technologies represent important elements in student learning. Why shouldn't the campus organization charged with this task structure its work as it sees best and hand over to others the results of student interaction with information and its systems? No one organization can accomplish all that is required for teaching and learning.

If the library were *sui generis* and if information were a phenomenon that existed separately from whatever might be done with it on campus, I would agree. The library could be the information franchise on campus, managing and dispensing an independently sourced commodity, which would be used by teachers and students as they thought it necessary to avail themselves of it. But, of course, such is not the case. Information—formally recorded and organized knowledge—is the material with which students learn and teachers teach.

The content of teaching and learning on campus is the "library." That is, the library is the repository for the accumulated knowledge communicated in teaching and acquired in learning. As such, its collection, organization, access, manipulation, and interpretation should lie fully in the hands of those charged with managing learning through the curriculum on campus. The rise of professionalization with and in the library and its workers has over the years led to increasing distance between the collection and management of this learning content and those charged with teaching and mastering it. One result of this alienation has been that the decisions about the content of the library is vested largely with librarians, those who have little idea of what materials will actually be used in "classroom" learning (because they are unfamiliar with course syllabi and teacher intentions) or how they will be used for this (because they are unfamiliar with the pedagogies in the various courses).

Of course, over the years, methods have been developed to try to reintegrate the library's content with learning, from the library's side. Library use instruction evolved into bibliographic instruction, which has become, largely, information literacy. In the latter, however, there are no consistency of thought and action and no widely accepted theoretical foundation. Depending on the circumstances, it can mean simply library and bibliographic use instruction on steroids or an effort to teach students how to search for information and manipulate the associated technology, or occasionally it can be an effort to assume some of the responsibility of the teacher to provide meaning and context to the information in play in the classroom.

These types of activities, along with traditional reference service, represent the library's efforts to discharge what it sees as its responsibility for the use of the materials it has collected or to which it provides access. The library, in other words, is taking its content and attempting to move into the instructional space owned by the faculty and the curriculum. Much is made of the need for partnerships between librarians and teachers and the need to integrate what the library does with the classroom. Underlying this activity, and especially bound up with an understanding of information literacy, is the idea of a very large body of information "out there," existing in many forms and growing exponentially. Learners need to be able to find what is useful for their learning in this mass and librarians will provide the instruction needed to do this. Some of it will be in the local library but most of it will not, and students need to know how to get to it independently, and, having reached it, must learn how to appropriate it and integrate the relevant content into their learning. I submit that without the classroom's direction and insight, without an understanding of meaning and context, without being able to read the material adequately and write about it well, we do students an injustice by teaching them to find information they cannot understand or appropriate properly.

The answer to this dilemma is to place the library directly under the control of the curriculum and to make it an instrument of teaching and learning, operationalized through the syllabi and first-day instructions of the various courses. In this way, the library no longer serves as a mediator of information to teaching and learning but becomes the agent of teachers and students into information. That is, the content of the library is determined largely by empirically demonstrable teaching and learning requirements rather than by professional librarian-developed criteria, which are largely unconnected to "classroom" learning activities. McDonald and Micikas (1990) offer an example of how this can be done using course syllabi to derive criteria for materials selection in the hands of instructors.

However, this is only one piece of the reestablished library. Designing an organization for the more important elements of student activity in the library—disciplinary reading and writing skills, making sense of retrieved information, and learning to critique information technology—puts us into new territory in academia and one which, potentially, will lead to a set of activities largely replacing those now associated with the library and create the need for a successor organization addressing those requirements, even though certain library-like activities (the acquisition or accessing, organization, and management of content) will continue. The last section of this article examines some of the opportunities and possible problems of this new wineskin for the new wine of the integration of learning and information as directed by teaching and learning.

THE NEW WINESKIN

Three questions concern us here: (1) What might be the shape and activities of this new organization; do we get there from here by evolutionary stages or by a revolutionary design *de novo*? (2) How will it differ from what we now know as the academic library? (3) How will we assess the effect of this organization's activities on learning?

I need to stress at this point that, before trying to define and design a solution, the host institution needs to agree on the scope and extent of the problem and the proposed solution. Specifically, this means that teachers and appropriate administrators must be fully informed about the problem and persuaded that the solution will achieve the desired ends without damaging the academic budget. Provosts, in particular, will likely be skeptical at first and, if an evolutionary change of uncertain duration seems to be the best way to go, will look for strong controls on the project and a strong manager to design and direct the effort. The library director may not be the individual best suited for this, but may need to accept a lesser role on a design and implementation team whose director comes from the faculty. The end result, of course, may not be simply a redesigned set of library services, but rather an organization that will eventually or maybe immediately serve as an academic instructional unit addressing significant educational needs.

And that defines the difficulty in trying to give shape and form to a refounded library. The first concern needs to be for an institutional agreement on the scope of the problem, which requires some understanding of what the present library can and cannot do, what the present library is and is not.

A way to approach the "library problem" is to frame it in terms of the needs of the increasing numbers of poorly prepared students now arriving on campus and the lack of learning in their first two years there. An extensive discussion of this issue is beyond the scope of this article. However, a thorough, empirically based study and discussion of the matter is found in Arum and Roksa (2011). The key finding in their study was that in the first two years of college, 45 percent of students surveyed showed no improvement in a widely used measure of learning achievement, the Collegiate Learning Assessment (CLA). As the authors state, "Growing numbers of students are sent to college at increasingly higher costs, but for a large proportion of them the gains in critical thinking, complex reasoning and written communication are either exceedingly small or empirically nonexistent" (121).

Another good introduction and guide to the issues of these students is Bauerlein's *The Dumbest Generation* (2008). He defines and documents the deficiencies and inabilities of the "web generation" with painstaking detail. It is possible, of course, that in any given institution, circumstances are not as grim as Bauerlein describes. At highly selective and academically demanding colleges, students may arrive well-prepared for college work. This does not vitiate the need for a reestablished library. However, the argument for this will have to be made along the lines of improving an already good phenomenon, rather than creating a solution to a set of seemingly intractable problems.

In my view, conditions of student learning in higher education argue for an aggressive approach to reformulating the academic library; in this redesign, an organization will emerge bearing little resemblance to today's academic library. Below, I describe such an organization.

There are, of course, many possible variants to this, and each institution will need to decide what is best suited to its mission and values. However, an early attempt at a uniform design and set of activities across institutions, emerging, for example from an ACRL task force promulgating a set of standards, would be unfortunate and unlikely to move the "profession" far enough along in a timely way. The issues in play are, of course, larger than parochial library ones. It is better to have many institutions "beta testing" solutions that vary according to their needs. These are more likely to receive sympathy from regional accreditors, who will be interested in solutions to academic and administrative problems specific to a college, rather than in the implementation of a one size fits all standard model, which continues the largely lockstep approach to academic library design and activity of the twentieth century.

Although I hope a more apt expression may emerge, for now, I call this new organization the Information and Learning Center (ILC). It is established as a laboratory for the entire curriculum and brings together in one place, around a common mission and set of objectives, the institution's commitment to its students in reading, writing, enumeration, and finding and using information. Its purpose is not remediation. Rather, it exists to extend a teacher's pedagogy in those areas of teaching and learning that cannot be addressed realistically in most classrooms. It is not reading, writing, and math added to the library. Instead, it is the "library" added to these activities.

Reading and writing are the two most basic information seeking and handling skills. Unless a student can read with insight and understanding, discern context, intent, and point-of-view, and, when necessary, read in the various disciplines according to the standards and protocols of that discipline, they have not "accessed" information, no matter the searching and machine manipulation skills they may employ. Likewise with writing. A student who cannot write well (or speak or present well) has not mastered the content of information. Reading, writing, and enumeration, as related to information-seeking, are a single but complex act of intellectual development and cannot be disaggregated without damaging learning. The learning of many college students is, to a greater or lesser degree, thus damaged. From the very beginning, the ILC will have a different mission from that of a library. The ILC will be established as an extension of the classroom, under the direction of the curriculum and individual instructors' pedagogies. The activities of the ILC will be supervised by the Curriculum Committee and be designated an instructional, rather than a support, unit of the institution. It will, of course, have its own support infrastructure, a considerably reduced library-like support staff.

Collection and management of materials, access to information, and "information literacy" activities will not be the mission of the organization. Rather the mission will be to teach students how to bring their learning needs and information materials together for learning, and to teach students the skills they lack to do this successfully. This will not preclude students and teachers from using the ILC for what might be seen as traditional library activities: general book and periodical reading, printing and photocopying, "circulation" services. However, these will be seen as subordinate and ancillary activities. Collections and services will be established and elaborated for the learner's needs, not the "library users" needs. There will be no "reference services." Rather, students will use the library in the context of their curriculum- and classroom-directed learning and in consultation with appropriate faculty and specialists. Materials will be selected based on learning (and teaching) requirements, with empirically demonstrable connections to students' learning needs through teachers' syllabi (McDonald and Micikas 1990).

The most visible difference between a library and an ILC will be in the absence of information literacy activities. However, the ILS staff and associated faculty will teach students how to find information in the context of specific learning needs and goals and to use this information in learning, as well as how to use and critique information technology in education and the culture generally, rather than merely to uncritically and thoughtlessly assume its presence and operation. Information literacy in libraries, at present, is a thoroughly mixed bag of efforts that range from simple library use instruction to well-meant attempts to assume for the library a role in learning for which it is not well prepared. In any event, it addresses information, not learning, and the ILC will concern itself with learning before information.

The ideal "professional" to work with students across these aspects of learning is someone I call tentatively an Information and Learning Specialist (ILS), a new kind of educator, with graduate training including the doctorate, to address these issues together with the student. This person will have mastered, at minimum, the teaching of reading and writing, information manipulation, and the interplay among these activities. Given the lack of rigor in much of our tertiary education, it is likely unrealistic to expect such a person also to be able to incorporate math teaching skills in the mix. Perhaps, however, I underestimate the abilities of contemporary graduate students. One possible source for this specialist is the large number of graduate students now unable to find employment in academia and the large pool of adjunct faculty in the system.

Another approach to staffing the ILC is to creatively use existing faculty appointments. In large lecture classes, instructors can do little more than lecture. Instead of having four instructors each lecturing classes of forty five students, an academic division would have two teachers lecturing ninety students each and two professors "seconded" to the ILS, to extend the activities of the lecture classroom into the ILS for small group and individualized learning activities as needed. All four instructors would coordinate their activities among themselves to assure that all 180 students would receive adequate attention. If an institution decided to take an evolutionary approach to the development of its ILC, it would be relatively easy to pilot an approach such as described above, while maintaining traditional library services.

A broader example may help clarify what will happen in the ILC and illustrate the difference between an ILC and a library. In many colleges, entering students are expected to enroll in a course or courses that address the fundamentals of reading, writing, and perhaps some aspects of literature. Typically, these are 100-level English courses, although they may be combined with the larger first-year student experience set of activities. In many of these and related courses, there are writing assignments for which the student is expected to "go to the library" for the sources to be used in completing the assignment. Many, perhaps most, students have little idea of how to "use" the library or how to write an academic paper or how to properly read documents. The library may offer some "help," usually quite insufficient to adequately meet the student's needs. Meanwhile, the "classroom" will focus on the student's reading and writing skills, broadly, and leave the "library skills" to be taught by the library staff.

Although one can find examples of where "rhetoric" courses succeed, the more usual experience is that they do not work well. And, how can they, when a single instructor is working with twenty-five to thirty students, most of whom cannot read, write, or think critically about their own experiences, let alone the content of classroom instruction or that of academic and scholarly publishing? The problem is not limited, of course, to beginning English students. The problem is endemic throughout the curriculum. If they are to be considered truly educated, students must be able to "converse" in the various disciplines, which require reading, writing, and critical judgment according to a discipline's ways of thinking about "its" phenomena and the protocols it uses to communicate "its" ideas. Little of this is taught and learned in liberal arts institutions. To learn it well requires the student be able to integrate learning and information skills with the content of the various disciplines, to manipulate ideas, to engage in metacognition (thinking about his or her own thinking), and by so doing develop the insight, which with practice and experience yields wisdom.

The information and learning center, with a faculty of appropriately trained information and learning specialists, is conceived as the "place" (however, it does not have to be fixed in a separate building), where these skills can be learned. The pedagogies practiced by the information and learning specialists will emerge from the confluence of the content of a discipline with the skills and techniques needed to move with assurance in the content, much like the pedagogies used in a laboratory of a laboratory science. "Classroom" and ILC specialists will hold complementary responsibilities for leading the student's learning, with a greater or lesser involvement of the instructor specialist, depending upon the learning needs of the student.

Instructional techniques will vary by discipline and institutions, but will likely range from individualized learning experiences to large group presentations. By persistently meeting with each other, individually or in groups, instructors and specialists will assure themselves and the student that the learning experiences in the "classroom" and the ILC are integrated. In this way the "content" of the library evolves into the content of learning, rather than a "collection," which may or may not be used for learning. Staff effort is directed toward the support of learning, not to the support of "library services." Cataloging is focused on developing learning-driven access to content, not on rationalizing the formal corpus of the world's accumulated knowledge.

In an ILC, some traditional library-like activities will necessarily remain. Materials would have to be purchased, processed, shelved, and "circulated." Licenses for digital subscriptions would have to be negotiated. Systems would have to be maintained. Someone would have to be designated to support the center's digital contents. None of this, however, requires master's level training. A bachelor's degree in information systems would be entirely adequate. Existing library-degreed staff will have several options, depending on what they are now doing. They can learn the skills and approaches to learning needed to become an information and learning specialist by returning to school or, perhaps, through an institution-wide librarian development program that will use existing professors and outside assistance as needed, perhaps in concert with area colleges moving in the same direction.

One approach to developing suitable staff for the ILC would be to begin with a pilot program, staffed by existing teachers, each, perhaps, given released time. Assuming this pilot is successful, three activities could begin simultaneously: librarians would begin development activities, more existing professors would be brought into the program, and an institution would begin exploring with other colleges and universities ways to equip adjuncts and unemployed graduate students with the specialist skills, drawing on the growing experiences of ILCs in other institutions. At the same time, planning could begin to establish a new degree program, possibly by reforming existing "library schools" into programs to train the ILS. Alternatively, existing graduate programs in education or English could consider adding programs for the preparation of ILC specialists.

How will an institution assess the ILC's relationship and contributions to learning? As anyone who has worked with institutional accreditation knows, there are no meaningful ways to assess a library's contribution to student learning success. It is possible to assess a library's organizational effectiveness, and this is what most frequently is presented for institutional regional accreditation. But, exactly what does a library contribute to learning, other than "support" it well?

In an ILC, however, student learning will be associated with the curriculum and specific course objectives and outcomes. The content of learning can be assessed through rubrics that will measure the extent and quality of ILC-related course learning activities. The success of the ILC as an organization can then be assessed on separate organizational-derived criteria, similar to any other administrative unit.

College libraries are at a critical juncture in their history and that of American higher education, generally. Many libraries have chosen to build a future by attempting to know that future and to stake their future on a largely uncritical and unexamined faith in information and its technologies.

This leaves the students in these libraries' sponsoring institutions in a difficult place with respect to their learning. Acquiring information is not learning and by itself is of no benefit to learning—the reason students enroll in colleges.

Libraries are established on the assumption that they are an integral part of learning. As long as they remain based on information and technology, they cannot be an integral part of collegiate learning. The answer to this dilemma lies in moving libraries onto a foundation that subordinates information to teaching and learning activities conducted at the intersection of learning and information. This will likely lead to a new type of academic organization, the information and learning center, staffed with teachers and information and learning specialists whose work with students is assessed as a necessary part of curricular and course learning assessment.

REFERENCES

Arum, R., and J. Roksa. 2011. *Academically adrift: Limited learning on college campuses*. Chicago: University of Chicago Press.

Bauerlein, M. 2008. The dumbest generation: How the digital age stupefies young Americans and jeopardizes our future (or, don't trust anyone under 30). New York: Tarcher.

Bennett, S. 2003. *Libraries designed for learning*. Washington: Council on Library and Information Resources. http://www.clir.org/pubs/reports/pub122/contents.html.

Berry, Wendell. 2005. *Starting by words*. Berkeley, CA: Shoemaker & Hoard.

McDonald, J., and L. Micikas. 1990. Collection evaluation and development by syllabus analysis: The must-ought-could (MOC) method at Holy Family College. In *Acquisitions '90: Conference on acquisitions, budgets and collections: May 16 and17, 1990, St. Louis, Missouri: Proceedings*, ed. D. C. Genaway, 289–316. Canfield, OH: Genaway.

Staley, D. J., and K. J. Malenfant. 2010. *Futures thinking for academic librarians: Higher education in 2025*. Chicago: Association of College and Research Libraries. http://www.ala.org/ala/mgrps/divs/acrl/issues/value/futures2025.pdf.

Other People's Money: Adapting Entrepreneurial Techniques to Build Capital in Challenging Economic Times

ROBERT FARRELL

Leonard Lief Library, Lehman College, CUNY, Bronx, New York, USA

Drawing on the "predator" model of entrepreneurship put forward by Villette and Vuillermot in their 2009 book "From Predators to Icons," this article argues that challenging economic times reveal that self-funded, collaborative information literacy models have in many cases unsustainably overstretched staff and budgets. In such circumstances, it is necessary for librarians to shift to an entrepreneurial approach that seeks profitable opportunities funded by parties other than the library in order to build capital for current and future instructional services. Following Villette and Vuillermot, the article seeks to refute a cultural myth that sees the entrepreneur as someone who is first and foremost a "do-gooder" or marketer of helpful products, and it also advocates that librarians adopt a view of the entrepreneur as one who preys on unexploited, low-cost/high-profit opportunities to leverage "other people's money" to build capital for later innovation. The article considers the economics of information literacy and library instruction programs, provides historical context for what has come to be known as the "collaborative imperative," points to the economic shortsightedness of many collaborative and "embedded librarian" partnerships, and details six examples from information literacy programs that model successful entrepreneurship of the sort argued for.

In line with the general goals of all information literacy (IL) programs, recent literature on college and university IL services has emphasized models of collaborative and embedded librarianship as ways of expanding instructional offerings and learning opportunities to as comprehensive a group of students as possible (Mounce 2010). A "collaborative imperative" has been recognized and responded to by college libraries due to a number of historical factors leading to a necessary increase in IL services. Iannuzzi's well-cited 1998 article, "Faculty Development and Information Literacy: Establishing Campus Partnerships," in which she promotes strategies for creating partnerships on college campuses that extend IL instruction into the disciplines and various other programs such as college writing centers, early college initiatives, etc., is characteristic of this push toward academic library collaboration. More recently, Shumaker et al.'s work to popularize the concept of embedded librarianship has become central to many models of IL instruction (2007, 2010). More and more libraries are dedicating more and more time to disciplinary instruction, often working with individual courses as much as the disciplinary faculty paid to teach those credit hours.

These approaches have helped move IL from the library into the curriculum. They reflect an admirable educational impulse. But they have also created a tension within libraries between the objective of increasing student learning opportunities and the financial and temporal realities that face our instructional programs, especially in challenging economic times. We have seemed to push aside the fact that current forms of innovative partnership rely on a high initial outlay of resources—what we might think of as capital, both financial and human—on the part of libraries, typically in the form of staff or faculty time and the transfer of resources from one service area to another.

In short, we haven't asked a simple question: How can we sustain our growing financial commitments to IL programs over the long term? How do we pay for it? In many respects, we've created a large number of unfunded mandates for ourselves, programs that during flush times are manageable but that become unsustainable when the economy falters, budgets shrink, and finite librarian work hours have to be stretched to cover noninstructional services. One thinks here of libraries that have had to lay off adjunct reference or instruction librarians or other contingent labor, shifting workloads and responsibilities to already maxed-out full-time staff. There will, of course, be those who believe that our IL mandates are not "unfunded" but are simply new responsibilities that should be paid for by increasing librarian "productivity," that is to say, by doing more in the same amount of time and for the same amount of money. To a point, this is true, and productivity can be improved. However, given the real increase in instructional workload and the very real complaints about the quantity of teaching in which librarians are engaged, it is a fact that many IL programs have become overstretched due to poor financial planning and the extension of instructional services without the resources needed to sustainably do so.

Shumaker's column in *Reference and User Services Quarterly* touches on this fact, noting that the "resource effects" involved in developing and sustaining embedded librarian projects can be "substantial" (2009, 242). In challenging economic times, Shumaker's suggestions for mitigating resource effects—dropping activities to save money, requesting funds from administration, asking the customer to pay directly for embedded services they may have received for free, that is to say, on the library's dime—can be difficult if not impossible. What then are instruction programs and the librarians who manage them to do?

Drawing on the "predator" model of entrepreneurship put forward by Villette and Vuillermot in their 2009 book *From Predators to Icons*, this article will argue that challenging economic times require a shift to an interim entrepreneurial approach that seeks profitable opportunities funded by parties other than the library in order to build capital for future expenditure. While many librarians have attempted to adopt entrepreneurial approaches in the area of IL program development, they tend to see the entrepreneur as someone who is fundamentally an innovator, someone who looks for opportunities to introduce and expand needed or desired services in order, like Preston Tucker and his "car of the future," to benefit human kind (Tucker 2000). In short, we have bought into a myth that sees the entrepreneur as someone who is first and foremost a "do-gooder." From this standpoint, the entrepreneur is simply a marketer of sorts who gets people to want some great, good thing he's manufactured at his own expense.

Contrary to this myth, Villette and Vuillermot argue, entrepreneurs are not big risk takers willing to gamble their own resources for the sake of doing good in the world. Rather, they are risk averse and engage in what they call "predation." Entrepreneurs aim for the "sure thing," as Gladwell notes in his recent review of their book (2010, 24). They look for unexploited, low-cost/high-profit opportunities, and they find ways to use other people's money to build capital for their own later innovation. In libraries, new collaborative services should be thought of as innovations. Innovations, the authors argue, are "collective" endeavors that require partners. But more importantly, the authors remind us, collaborative work—innovation—is a "luxury you have to be able to afford" (Villette and Vuillermot, 84). The true entrepreneur knows that he first needs capital if he is to undertake new ventures or introduce new services.

Villette and Vuillermot's argument is simple: "one grows rich through innovating only on condition of having previously acquired the means of controlling the innovation and of being able to resist subsequent uncertainties," such as difficult economic times. "Mastery of innovation presupposes the control of sufficient financial resources and of a network of alliances enabling the distribution of expense and risk" (84). Translated into the world of academic libraries, Villette and Vuillermot's thesis tells us that libraries must adopt a truly entrepreneurial attitude if instructional services are to become more economically sustainable and if we are to weather recessionary periods. We must look to build the needed capital and distribute financial risk (both in the form of money and time) among partners outside the library before introducing innovative collaborative services. And if we have already over-extended ourselves, we must attempt to increase our capital to cover current services and put ourselves in a position to continue growing our services in more viable ways going forward. Again, innovation is a luxury you have to be able to afford. For too long, libraries have ignored this fact and they are now faced with cutting instructional services or asking already overburdened librarians to teach more as others are pulled in different directions or let go for budgetary reasons.

There are several historical and institutional reasons that have led us to heed the collaborative imperative without heeding the need to prudently build capital. I'll begin by considering these factors. I'll then clarify Villette and Vuillermot's portrait of the entrepreneur as predator and outline the steps of successful predation. In so doing, three projects recently undertaken in lieu of expanding existing collaborative relationships at Lehman College (City University of New York), projects that have avoided costs while maximizing "capital" accumulation, will be presented as examples of successful predation. Along with these projects, I will present several examples from other academic libraries. I'll conclude with a consideration of the social and psychological factors that may hinder librarians from adopting this needed predatory approach.

WHY COLLABORATE? "THE COLLABORATIVE IMPERATIVE"

To begin, let us state that the "collaborative imperative," the perceived need for librarians to work with faculty across disciplines to ensure that students are able to locate, evaluate, and use information intelligently, is a real imperative. I've adopted this phrase from the title of Raspa and Ward's *The Collaborative Imperative: Librarians and Faculty Working Together in the Information Universe* (2000) as much for its truth as for the sense of frantic urgency its title and much of its contents convey. As IL professionals, we know that our instruction is important if students are to succeed in the academic world as well as in the larger world outside the academy. Yet, what is it about this imperative that has led librarians to rush into collaborative relationships without first securing the necessary resources to do so? What has led us to initiate, in what retrospectively seems an almost headlong way, so many unfunded IL mandates? While the real needs of students have driven the growth of IL services, the haste in which it has been accomplished and the correlate lack of financial forethought can be seen as a result of a kind of felt "existential threat" to the profession as a whole and the need to make our services tangibly and immediately relevant.

Between the late-1980s and mid-1990s, a variety of pressures began pushing librarians to rethink traditional models of bibliographic instruction. First, with the rise of new information technologies and the seeming ubiquity of information, teaching students how to utilize the physical spaces and resources of libraries through a single or small number of "one-shot" lessons no longer seemed adequate (Association of College and Research Libraries 1989). At the same time as this technological shift was occurring, college accreditors began emphasizing IL as a core learning objective across disciplines, introducing additional external pressures (Commission on Higher Education 1994; Ratteray 2002; Thompson 2002).

Third, following in the footsteps of John Dewey and other educational theorists, higher education in general began to shift to what has come to be called a "learner centered" model of instruction. Often cited as a seminal article in this area is Barr and Tagg's 1995 piece in *Change*, "From Teaching to Learning," in which the authors contrast the traditional "instruction paradigm" with what they called a "learner paradigm": college instruction that views the professor as an "inter-actor," someone who seeks to "elici[t] students' discovery and construction of knowledge" rather than simply someone who transfers his or her own knowledge to students (16). Shortly after the publication of Barr and Tagg's article, the influential report *Reinventing Undergraduate Education*, more commonly known as the *Boyer Report* (1998), was published. The report strongly advocated for a renewed attention to inquiry-based learning. While the *Boyer Report* only mentions libraries in passing, many librarians used the report and the general trend of the period as an opportunity to advance new inquiry-based initiatives requiring cross campus collaborations (Hensley 2006, 56–57; Thompson 2002; Watts 2008, 1).

Finally, after many years of cross-institutional conversation, the Association of College and Research Libraries issued its *Information Literacy Competency Standards for Higher Education* (2000), which set the bar for what students graduating from institutions of higher education ought to know and be able to do after completing their courses of study. Those accrediting agencies that hadn't yet issued formal guidelines for student IL performance did so shortly thereafter.

In response to these historical and institutional pressures, librarians began advocating for increased cooperation and collaboration across the disciplines and across the campus in order to give students the learning opportunities needed to meet these new perceived and mandated IL learning objectives. By 2000, Cook (2000) counted over four hundred articles published on the topic of librarian/disciplinary faculty collaborations and collaborations between various administrative and support service units and librarians. Iannuzzi's article was not the first to describe how to create successful, large-scale IL collaborations, but its emphasis on strategies aimed at influencing cultural changes favorable for IL initiatives in colleges and universities embodied a trend that seemed to reach a kind of critical mass at the time, while also exemplifying some of Rader's work from the period (1999). To this day, the topic remains important (Cochrane and Goodman 2009; Mackey and Jacobson 2005; Watts 2008).

These are real trends, and the pressures on libraries to supplement disciplinary instruction to help students become productive, independent inquirers have pushed librarians to expand IL services. However, an underlying fifth factor needs to be acknowledged. Unmentioned in the prevailing story of the rapid expansion of instructional services is the latent fear that new information technologies may in some way put librarians in the position of becoming obsolete, a fear that I believe has contributed to the haste and lack of financial forethought when it comes to IL program planning.

Two articles in the January 1996 issue of the *Journal of Academic Librarianship* seem to point to this worry. Wegner's brief op-ed, "Is it True What They Say?: The Library on a Credit Card," aims to refute a notion the author states in two concise sentences: "By the year 2000, books will be obsolete and the whole library will be accessible on a credit card! Library use will be entirely self-directed, with no librarian intervention necessary!" (51) Her conclusion is that libraries will continue to be needed because "librarianship ... is about making appropriate choices of resources and organizing that material into an intellectual whole. This requires space and persons. Because more and more, librarianship is about teaching, guiding, and interpreting" (52). Teaching students to be information literate is, in a sense, the thing that's going to keep librarians employed. Rider's article, "Developing New Roles for Paraprofessionals in Cataloging," is fascinating as a companion piece to Wegner's, for it seems to provide the historical context for the fears of reference and instruction librarians at the time. Rider's piece points to the ways automation and technological innovations led libraries to downsize or completely eliminate professional cataloging positions in favor of paraprofessional labor or altogether outsourcing cataloging activities. The trend Rider points to is one that began in the 1960s and has been discussed in the literature since then (Preston 1984).

Fears about librarian obsolescence are not unique to the mid-1990s, but a look at the literature does reveal those fears to be quite prevalent. Librarians continue to feel the pressure of justifying their jobs in the face of new technologies (Bivens-Tatum 2010; Huwe 2004). The rapid expansion of instructional services has, whether consciously or unconsciously, been one of the means to do so.

ENTREPRENEURIAL ADVICE?

As a result of these factors—the real needs of students, the pressures of accreditation and formalization of IL standards, and the real fear of what might happen if we did not justify our presence on college campuses—librarians were encouraged to adopt an "entrepreneurial" approach in order to expand

IL services. Booth and Fabian (2002) advise librarians "to adopt a strategic, forward-looking, entrepreneurial approach for integrating the library agenda into institutional documents and for making IL a centerpiece of university success measures." (139) For them, the IL "entrepreneur" would seem to be someone capable of identifying unexploited markets and IL "needs" in order to thereby create new policies or services that give shape to those markets or fulfill those needs. Librarians in this scenario are encouraged to be creative "innovators," similar to those in the for-profit business world who identify new needs and demands and thereby invent products or services that bring profit to inventors and market innovators.

By "entrepreneurial," Booth and Fabian certainly do not mean the kind of external entrepreneurship advocated for by Neal in his 2001 article documenting the many "for-profit" business ventures established by the Johns Hopkins University Libraries. Rather, Booth and Fabian seem to equate entrepreneurship with a kind of marketing. In other words, they see entrepreneurship as an activity that seeks to promote and extend current services rather than an activity that is aimed at generating profits. This equation of entrepreneurship and marketing in the context of collaboration seems to be a common line of thought in academic librarian discourse (e.g., Bell 2009; Currie and Eodice 2005, 45).

In our efforts to respond quickly and comprehensively to the collaborative imperative, in our efforts to expand the scope of our instructional services, we've forgotten to ask how we intend to pay for these services, and, perhaps more importantly, how we will sustain and continue to grow them when budgets shrink. When it comes to finding the funds to pay for library services, ACRL (2006) advises that librarians frame to those holding the purse-strings how bad things will be and what various stakeholders will lose out on if funding is not provided for various services. The document does not address ways of developing programs that are profitable and self-sustaining. Its primary objective seems to be to make librarians into effective marketers of library services. However, this proves ineffective when campus budgets are cut across the board.

Academic libraries simply have not addressed the issue of funding IL services. A recent study of strategic IL planning in higher education analyzes documentation from a number of major universities for "key themes of information literacy strategy" (Corrall 2008, 31). While themes such as "Embed [IL] in curricula," "Work with others," and "Raise awareness [of IL services]" are readily identifiable, the author does not present evidence of strategic thinking in the area of resource acquisition. The financial costs of expanding IL services do not seem to be included in library planning and correlately have not been addressed in the literature.

Shumaker's (2009) suggestions for embedded library programs to cope with challenging economic times also belie an initial lack of strategic forethought. His advice to "charge-back" departments for already existing services is likely unfeasible for most academic libraries and to attempt to introduce it would perhaps even be politically damaging. Shumaker and Tyler note in 2007 that funding is a "challenge" for academic librarian embedded collaboration (7), and he points out that, unlike corporate or other special libraries, academic embedded services are not "funded by the customer" but rather "centrally managed and centrally funded" by the libraries themselves (21). His 2009 article's warning about "failing to allocate adequate funding and staff resources . . . , inadequate attention to workload leveling . . . , and overlooking the threats to library staff cohesion" (242), seems to be retrospective advice and leaves those planning future collaborative relationships with little practical guidance on avoiding the pitfalls of which he warns. In the absence of corporate-like funding models, academic librarians don't need to have the obvious consequences of overstretching library budgets and staff pointed out to them. We see this every day. Rather, we need strategic plans for figuring out how to fund embedded and collaborative relationships.

The first strategic step is to recognize that such collaborations may ultimately lead to deficits in difficult economic times. One must know that this is a possibility ahead of time, think about the collaborative relationship in terms of its long-range impact, and look for ways to carry the costs of those services that cannot be abandoned either for educational or political reasons. Too often collaborations are undertaken under the sway of immediate exigencies and for the sake of short-term "profits," such as meeting pressing accreditation demands, with little regard for their cost over the long run. The second step is for libraries to truly become entrepreneurial rather than simply creating more and more demand for their finite instructional supply, that is to say, librarian work hours. We must therefore have a clear conception of what characterizes entrepreneurial behavior. Entrepreneurship is not marketing. It is predation.

PREDATORS VS. DO-GOODERS

Villette and Vuillermot show that a myth has been built up around the notion of the "entrepreneur," blinding us to what entrepreneurs, or businessmen as the authors more prosaically choose to refer to them, really do. From the standpoint of the mythic conception of the entrepreneur, the "successfull businessm[a]n" is typically seen as "not only . . . a hero but as someone who sacrifices himself for the common good, at the risk of his life and fortune" (2). The word "entrepreneur," the authors point out, has connoted this myth among English speakers since it was first "introduced into economics by John Stuart Mill in 1848," who used it to refer to someone who "achieved something [or] accomplished a task": someone "through whom come prosperity and progress for the entire community" (19).

In other words, the myth is that the entrepreneur sees a need in society more clearly than others, sees the way to satisfy that social need, and then introduces innovative products or services, thereby transforming the world for the better. The entrepreneur is seen as a kind of noble "do-gooder," willing to risk his own capital or that of those who believe in his idea, for the sake of some social good.

For Villette and Vuillermot, the problem with this myth is that it has obscured how extremely successful business people, those who are known for their entrepreneurial spirit and for introducing socially beneficial innovations into the marketplace, positioned themselves to do so. Super-successful entrepreneurs start out not as heroes, but as risk-averse predators: ruthless business people whose sole aim is to accumulate as much capital as possible in the safest manner possible. Innovation only occurs after this phase of capital accumulation. This "successful businessman" is "constantly and almost exclusively on the lookout for opportunities to make profits higher than the cost of the capital he is using" (120). "In all stories of innovation," the author's write, "it is necessary to pay close attention to chronology: innovation occurs not at the beginning of prosperous business affairs but during them. Innovation follows other business deals that make it possible because they provide the outlet, the resources, and the funds. It is also because of these prior and preparatory business dealings that the businessman is able to grasp the full advantage of the inventions made by others, appreciate their potential value and, if possible, acquire them at low cost before that value has become known" (90).

By buying into the cultural myth of the entrepreneur, librarians have prioritized innovation and service growth while overlooking the need to first acquire the capital needed to implement such growth. Successful entrepreneurs may become "do-gooders" later in their lives or careers, but they usually don't start out as such. We must therefore rethink our conception of the entrepreneur if we are to regain our fiscal balance. The predator is someone who positions himself "'between' (*entre*) in order to 'take' (*prendre*)" (111).

HOW THE PREDATOR PREYS

Villette and Vuillermot follow many other theorists of entrepreneurship when they point out that successful entrepreneurs are typically those who have "made the most of unforeseen circumstances," (4), those who have "cleverly exploited exceptionally favorable business opportunities" (5). But the successful entrepreneur does not simply happen upon such opportunities, in their view. Rather, the "decisive operations" by which fortunes are made "chiefly ai[m] at recognizing, exploiting, creating or provoking market anomalies, momentary sources of large localized profits. In other words . . . [it is] essentially political work . . . " (103).

The authors continue to say that the predaceous entrepreneur is always looking for undervalued commodities or businesses, things he can cheaply acquire and quickly turn over for the potential profit he perceives. He is looking for companies in distress that he believes he can acquire and turn around for his own gain. He is looking for deals in which he will be the stronger player in the position of reaping the most reward while risking the least out of those involved. As Villette and Vuillermot write, the skilled entrepreneur has an informed "view of the current and potential value of activities of which they have direct knowledge and which they have the means to influence." By "market anomalies" the authors mean inefficiencies in the marketplace: areas of the market in which things are either over- or undervalued, the perception of which requires superior knowledge and insight.

In the following section, I will detail three IL ventures undertaken by the library for which I work. Each of these ventures required both aspects of successful predation outlined above: spotting a market anomaly ripe for exploitation and looking for ways to use other people's money, "capital" in the broad sense as we've defined it, to fund the venture. Three additional ventures from other libraries will serve to further illustrate the principles of predation Villette and Vuillermot describe.

To be clear, the "exploitation" here is not the kind of exploitation characteristic of the larger market place. No individuals unduly profited from these ventures in personal ways. Rather, the ventures yielded "profit" to the libraries in that they have positioned them to continue or expand these ventures or related ventures at little to no cost to the libraries. And if we wish to take this line of thinking farther, we can say that those who ultimately profited from these ventures are the students who received more extensive IL instruction than otherwise would have been available.

SEEING WHAT'S THERE 1: PREYING ON AN EXISTING COURSE

When first hired as the Coordinator of Information Literacy at Lehman College, the author examined the current course offerings throughout the various departments. Like all IL coordinators, the author found himself having to respond to the "collaborative imperative" and was looking for ways to extend our current IL reach, primarily through building relationships that would result in more course-embedded research sessions requested by disciplinary faculty. The author also came across an "introduction to college"-type course with a focus on online research listed under the Adult and Continuing Education Division. It had evidently been created many years prior by the division's Adult Degree Program, which offers a BA for nontraditional students returning to college. The course had ceased being offered.

Our library had never offered a for-credit IL course and we did not, at the time, seem to possess the kind of social capital needed to introduce such a course into the traditional BA program. However, it did seem feasible to set up a meeting with the Divisional Dean who oversaw the Adult Degree Program to discuss the possibility of the library reviving and reconceiving the course as a potentially useful class for new students to the program. When I approached the Chief Librarian, a position on our campus roughly equivalent to dean, with this idea, he suggested that the present moment might not be the best time to meet with the Divisional Dean. The Divisional Dean had been in his position for many decades and was due to retire in the coming year.

If we consider the two aspects that allow for successful predation, we can see that the library was positioned with an opportunity to do something that would be paid for by another campus entity. Since the course was offered through a department in a division separate from the library, whoever taught the course would be hired as an adjunct to teach the course at no cost to the library. In other words, here was an opportunity to undertake a venture, using someone else's money, which we would otherwise have thought of undertaking using our own money had circumstances and fiscal conditions allowed. Due to the Chief Librarian's insight into the current campus conditions, we also possessed information that allowed us to predict an impending anomaly in the "market." In our conversation, we recognized that the transition to the new dean would create an opportunity for us. That is to say, it would introduce a situation that we might be able to exploit rather than one requiring us to enter into a discussion with someone who had no incentive to innovate. Changes in corporate or institutional leadership often lead to shifts in corporate direction, shifts in strategy, and an openness to new ideas.

We therefore waited for the current dean to retire and approached the new dean with our proposal shortly after she received her appointment. Our strategy worked, and, with the guidance and input of the division and Adult Degree Program, we were able to retool the existing course on the books into something that would benefit the students of that department and give us a foot in the world of for-credit IL courses.

Consequently, the library gained a significant amount of profit, primarily in the form of social and political capital on campus. The success of creating a three-credit course that resulted in positive student outcomes has allowed us to be seen in a new light as an academic department capable of developing new curricula. We were able to see what was on the books and turn it into an opportunity.

SEEING WHAT'S THERE 2: PREYING ON A STRUCTURAL ANOMALY

LaGuardia Community College is a large urban institution located in Queens, New York, and is a part of the City University of New York. Over the past year, the library there was able to spot a structural anomaly in the course requirements for a number of majors and options (what most colleges would call "concentrations") that resulted from a change in the way science courses are offered at the college. By seeing what was already there, librarians created a two-credit course and obtained the funds to run the course; they are now in a position to guarantee student enrollment in their course while keeping their expenditure of human capital, in the form of work hours devoted to advertising the course, to a minimum. The librarians approached the campus Office of Institutional Research, which determined that over three thousand students were affected by the change. This became one of the main rationales by which they justified the creation of a new two-credit liberal arts IL course. Like other departments that create new courses, the library will receive a budgetary increase to pay for the instructor hired to teach the course. While the course constitutes a certain amount of "new work" for the library, it is work that is and will continue to be paid for by the college.

LaGuardia's library has long had a one-credit IL course. To sustain enrollment in that course, they developed strong ties with the college's advising department which has, over the years, funneled into that course students who need a single credit to fulfill a program requirement. They will continue to leverage that relationship in order to ensure enrollment in their new course without having to engage in extensive, time-consuming advertising to students and programs.

OTHER PROGRAMS IN NEED 1: PREYING ON A GROWING DISCIPLINE

As a member of the college's Academic Senate, the author first heard about a new program aimed at providing a crash course in business skills to liberal arts majors in need of practical training that was to be started using funds from a corporate grant. While semiautonomous, the program would be housed within and receive guidance from the college's business department.

A marketing-oriented instruction librarian would have approached the new program with an offer to provide course-based IL instruction or some sort of extracurricular workshops on business research. Neither of these was an option given our already large instructional program. While such offerings may have benefited students in some way, they would have eaten away at what little capital the library currently has by requiring us to invest library faculty time to schedule, plan, organize, and conduct workshops during hours already devoted to other vital tasks.

Rather than take this direction, the author used some of the social capital acquired through our successful (and profitable) collaboration with the Adult Degree Program by proposing to the coordinators of the new business program that the library create a course to support liberal arts students pursuing studies in business late in their college career. The coordinators of the program were intrigued by the idea, and the author drafted a mock course description and outline for a class on "competitive intelligence." After several more conversations with various stakeholders, we received an endorsement from the business department to develop a formal course proposal that could be sent to the college's Undergraduate Curriculum Committee. We subsequently did so and received a positive response from the chairperson of that committee who also suggested that the course be cross-listed with the business department itself, rather than offered solely under the aegis of the library, a very positive turn of events that we've since accomplished. By so doing, we believe we will more easily be able to attract students to the course since it will ultimately fit into the elective requirements for the Bachelor's of Business Administration degree rather than a course that has no degree impact, thus cutting down on any costs we may have incurred in time trying to get students to take the course.

Barring any unforeseen circumstances, by the time of this article's publication the course will have made its way through our College Curriculum Committee, and we foresee a positive outcome. Not surprisingly, however, we were initially met with a bit of confusion and skepticism by some of the stakeholders in the process. Since the library had never offered a course before, it took a few minutes for those hearing our proposal to realize that we are, in fact, a full academic department with librarians possessing full faculty status (something that helped us in this situation). It also helped that we could draw on the capital derived from the success of our recent collaboration with the Adult Degree Program to legitimate our venture.

Again, being aware of a change in the college's organization led us to see the initial anomaly we could use to our advantage. Monies for the course will have to be funded by the college budgeting process and will not come out of the library's existing personnel or other-than-personnel budget levels. A librarian will be hired to teach the course on an adjunct basis, which won't tap into existing funds. Just as in the previous case, it is the students who will be ultimate beneficiaries of this course. But we will also profit as well. On top of the additional social capital we hope to accrue for the purpose of continuing to develop new credit-bearing courses, there are other long-term benefits. We will profit down the road from our new relationship with the business department, a department that continues to grow, both in numbers of students and in importance to the college. Over the period of time spent developing the competitive intelligence course, the business department introduced a new graduate program. New changes to our institutional structure may give this department even more prominence than it currently has. What does that give us? With a three-credit business course in our department and additional library attention needed by the growing business department, we may be in a position to lobby for the creation of a business librarian position, someone who can teach the existing course as well as work to provide instruction within our other IL programs. This, in turn, will lessen the instructional load of current faculty, thus increasing the library's capital as understood in terms of faculty time able to be spent on various other projects.

OTHER PROGRAMS IN NEED 2: PREYING ON A NEW MAJOR

Immersion in the details of one's institution has been a common theme in the above examples. At the New York City College of Technology, a college also in the City University system, Information Literacy Librarian Maura Smale built political capital for her library by actively involving herself in campus committees and developing relationships, not solely for the purpose of developing collaborative relationships but also as a means of positioning herself to discover potentially exploitable opportunities. She did this in a number of ways.

When new to the campus, she volunteered to serve as a nonvoting member of her College Council's curriculum committee. Not only was she able to observe the process of new course initiatives from conception to approval, she got to know those serving on the committee in a more personal way, developing a set of personal relationships that could be tapped at some future point if opportunity arose. Second, her library, like most libraries, also has an active liaison program between librarians and academic departments that serves to facilitate collection development and identify departmental IL needs. Through the liaison program, she was able to get to know a variety of programs and the faculty teaching in those programs. Lastly, Maura became very involved in a variety of new technology initiatives, both on campus and within the larger university system, specifically by working on a new social media platform created by the university to facilitate intra- and inter-campus communication and by participating in new cross-campus teaching with technology committees. This latter activity positioned her to develop vocabularies and conceptual frameworks by which to understand and communicate more effectively with the technologically-oriented programs with whom she worked in her capacity as a librarian within her college.

In this case, unlike the previous examples we've considered, Maura did not have to approach an entity outside her library with a proposal, but was rather approached by the creators of a new program in Emerging Media Technologies (offered through a department that she serves as liaison) about the possibility of creating a course for their department. To someone observing this event from outside the circumstances of its engendering, it would appear as if Maura were simply lucky to have been in the right place at the right time. By being known as someone familiar with the needs of new technological programs and as someone with the ability to navigate a new course proposal through the campus approval process, Maura was able to be perceived as someone to whom the Emerging Media Technologies program would naturally turn when the program discovered it needed a new course in research methods for its students. A profitable situation presented itself to her, seemingly by chance. However, her work building the social capital needed to attract the opportunity was acquired deliberately and thereby allowed the opportunity to arise and be effectively exploited.

Like the two-credit course at LaGuardia Community College and the competitive intelligence course at Lehman College, the course at City Tech has a built in base of students freeing the library from having to spend resources attracting students. Other departments that have seen the effectiveness of the course are now developing distribution models that include the library's research methods course as an elective option, thus allowing the library to expand the number of sections of the course going forward.

OTHER PEOPLE'S MONEY 1: SPOTTING OPPORTUNITY IN A GRANT-FUNDED PROGRAM

Grant writing can be quite labor intensive. It requires a large investment of time and energy that otherwise could be devoted to other projects. Additionally, grant applications are "risky." The odds of a library getting a major grant for an IL project are not high. Not only is there a lot of competition, there is also a lot of variation in funding levels and grant availability from various sources.

One way to minimize one's risk and correlatively maximize one's profit is to "piggy back" on grant applications written by other departments or college administrative units. To do this, one need only be networked with the active grant writers on campus and attuned to the conversations being had in various departments and among your campus grants coordinator or development officer.

Another way to minimize risk is to approach those you know who have recently received grants to see if they may need any services or programming that can be paid for out of their grant-funded coffers. If those who have received grants have worked with you before or know of the work you do and the services you provide, it is not unlikely that they will get in touch to see if you might be able to help them out.

As a result of previous traditional IL collaborations, our library was able to provide two four-day summer workshops for a group of junior high school students enrolled in an early college program run through a combined middle and high school associated with the college. And it did not cost the library a dime in time or money. Like our previous examples, these workshops were of a sort that at one point might have been done "on the clock" as part of a librarian's required duties, thus preventing that librarian from engaging in other activities and consequently impacting the library's productivity. Rather, we were able to have the program pay for our services through the other department's grant monies.

The author had previously provided instruction for this school's students who had enrolled in a college-level course and had the opportunity to get to know the program coordinator who is based on our campus. Over several months the author learned more about the early college program from her and was able to share with her some of the ideas that form the foundations of our IL program. She mentioned, in the course of our conversations, that she was in need of programming during the summer as part of her efforts to keep the junior high school students engaged and help them start thinking about the college-level courses they'd be taking in a few short years. The library was able to offer its services without hesitation, knowing that she would be able to fund any workshops we provided out of her own budget. Again, this saved the library from having to allot time and resources to an additional, unforeseen project. As an added bonus, a campus leader from the college's writing center was brought in to the project, which resulted in solidifying a budding partnership between her department and the library, a relationship that has since continued to bear fruit.

Like the previous examples, we relied on market knowledge to spot an anomaly ripe for "exploitation." If we had not come to know this program coordinator and been aware of her grant-funded project, or had not been attuned to her program's needs, this opportunity would have never been spotted. Knowing that there was a pool of operating money within the program allowed us to receive direct compensation for planning, as well as teaching, the workshops.

Again, those who profited most were the students who went through these workshops. But the library has accrued additional profits, both short and long term. As a result of undertaking this venture, the library and college writing center have developed new joint instructional programs. In addition, we recently presented some of our observations about the learning continuum we've seen between junior high and college students at a city-wide teacher librarian conference. The library has also now established a model of collaboration that requires partners to bring capital to the table in order to fund certain kinds of IL services.

OTHER PEOPLE'S MONEY 2: SPOTTING OPPORTUNITY IN CAMPUS INCENTIVES

In addition to grant-funded programs, opportunities to acquire money for library operations can be found by looking for various financial incentives tied to new campus initiatives. Our last example illustrates this technique and demonstrates that libraries can make "the most of unforeseen circumstances," to return to Villette and Vuillermot's phrase, to acquire monies that traditionally may be reserved for academic departments in the disciplines.

Like many institutions, the University of West Georgia (UWG), a school of about 11,500 undergraduate and graduate students, is feeling pressure to move more of its instruction into an online environment. It is a priority at the university as evidenced by the peer-reviewed journal, *The Online Journal of Distance Learning Administration*, published on campus. Anne Barnhart, Head of Instructional Services at the UWG library, and her colleagues discovered that their institution offers departments extra financial incentives to offer online courses. Students within their system pay a unique "etuition" rate for online courses, the proceeds of which are split among the distance education program, which receives 40 percent of each enrolled student's tuition, the department, which also receives 40 percent, and the administrative unit of the college, which receives the remaining 20 percent. Because the library is itself an administrative unit and a department, they are able to directly receive 60 percent of every student's tuition, 20 percent more than other departments, money that is designated by the university to enhance online teaching, learning, or other services. The money has been used to purchase hardware, including iPads used for online instruction, and their Libguides subscription.

In 2010, the library discovered that an additional incentive could be obtained by creating more advanced courses for students in the university's "honors" track. A department receives an additional $2500 for each honors course that it offers; these funds can be used for any purpose. The library offered its first section of an honor's IL course in the fall 2010 semester, and it was able to use the funds to increase their travel budget and purchase supplies needed to extend their outreach and promotional activities on campus, producing brochures and customized pens, in order to attract more students to their courses. They now hope to offer an honor's section each year, both in order to exploit the funds being offered and as a way to work with more advanced students and thereby develop their IL curriculum in new directions.

BECOMING A SUCCESSFUL PREDATOR

Librarians are not typically thought of as predators. But if we are to avoid continually collaborating in ways that overstretch our resources, we need to become so. It may be the case that we have seen less of this sort of approach in the nonprofit or academic world, primarily because these sorts of careers don't attract this kind of personality type. Those who are "other directed" or who gravitate to the security and sense of purpose that comes from being a part of a large, socially minded institution may not possess by nature the predator instinct needed to build capital and advance the positive educational agenda they value. Librarians are helpful, giving people. When there is a need or problem, we are trained to recognize it. Our instinct is to quickly try to satisfy or solve it. We want to supply the services that will give our "customers" the skills we know will serve them well. We want to expand our services through cross-disciplinary partnerships as quickly and as widely as we can. But we must do so in a calculated way, not hastily due to fears of becoming obsolete or looming accreditation requirements or the need to prove our own worth.

The ability to introduce new "products," develop new methods of service delivery, and integrate services into new markets requires the kind of capital, whether economic or social, needed to "fund" such ventures if those ventures aren't to bankrupt us or leave us without the capital needed to sustain other core services and operations. Researchers in the area of social entrepreneurship are beginning to look seriously at the issue of "profitability" and capital accumulation in order to give leaders in those fields new ways to think about the long-term viability of their services. We must do so, too.

As Villette and Vuillermot note, the successful business person "pursues his egotistical interests, adopts risky behavior, and speculates on uncertainty" in order to achieve his end of maximizing profits needed to fund current and future ventures (21). If we substitute the words "the students" or "his patrons" for "his egotistical," the above sentence sounds much more in line with our own values, for the personal interests of dedicated librarians truly are the same as those about whose educations we care. What is important to note in Villette and Vuillermot's observation is that it is necessary to operate in what we might call a moral "gray zone" if we are to advance our agenda and respond to the collaborative imperative in a sustainable and profitable way. "The entire difficulty," for the predatory entrepreneur, they conclude, "consists in combining the rapid accumulation of economic capital with the accumulation of symbolic capital—a good reputation in business" (110). But success begets success and positive results very often are remembered while the means by which they were attained forgotten. As Villette and Vuillermot point out, "The authority acquired by successfully accomplishing operation A can be reinvested in the form of a promise of success in a future operation B. A snowball effect can therefore be observed, success leading to a sort of symbolic credit facilitating the next success" (4).

While approaching collaborative innovation in the Machiavellian way described here may be distasteful to some, the capital that one can accrue by such methods is not acquired for the glory of one's IL program. It is accumulated in order to make our colleagues and ourselves less harried and overstretched. It is accumulated to give us more time to reflect, plan, and prepare. And, it is ultimately for our students who will profit from our renewed and sustained attention. The capital acquired by the predatory developer of IL programs is the source from which future opportunities for student success will be funded. In this way, growth through innovative collaborative partnerships becomes truly sustainable.

REFERENCES

Association of College and Research Libraries, American Library Association. 1989. Presidential committee on information literacy: Final report. http://www.ala.org/ala/mgrps/divs/acrl/publications/whitepapers/presidential.cfm.

———. 2000. Information literacy competency standards for higher education. http://www.ala.org/ala/mgrps/divs/acrl/standards/standards.pdf.

———. 2006. The power of personal persuasion: Advancing the academic library agenda from the front lines. http://www.ala.org/ala/mgrps/divs/acrl/issues/marketing/advocacy_toolkit.pdf.

Barr, R. B., and J. Tagg. 1995. From teaching to learning—a new paradigm for undergraduate education. *Change* 27:12–25.

Bell, S. J. 2009. The librarian entrepreneur? Demystifying an oxymoron. *Against the Grain* 21:18–20.

Bivens-Tatum, W. 2010. The lesson of library history. *Academic Librarian: On Libraries, Rhetoric, Poetry, History, & Moral Philosophy*, February 15. https://blogs.princeton.edu/librarian/2010/02/lesson_of_library_history.html.

Booth, A., and C. A. Fabian. 2002. Collaborating to advance curriculum-based information literacy initiatives. *Journal of Library Administration* 36:123–42.

Boyer Commission on Educating Undergraduates in the Research University. 1998. *Reinventing undergraduate education: A blueprint for America's research universities*. Stony Brook: State University of New York at Stony Brook. http://naples.cc.sunysb.edu/Pres/boyer.nsf/.

Cochrane, L. S., and V. D. Goodman, eds. 2009. Agility by design: Library collaborations across and beyond the campus. Special Issue, *College & Undergraduate Libraries* 16, nos. 2–3.

Commission on Higher Education, Middle States Association of Colleges and Schools. 1994. *Characteristics of excellence in higher education: Standards for accreditation*. Philadelphia: Commission on Higher Education, Middle States Association of Colleges and Schools.

Cook, D. 2000. Creating connections: A review of the literature. In *The Collaborative imperative: Librarians and faculty working together in the information universe*, ed. R. Raspa and D. Ward, 19–38. Chicago: Association of College and Research Libraries.

Corrall, S. 2008. Information literacy strategy development in higher education: An exploratory study. *International Journal of Information Management* 28:26–37.

Currie, L., and M. Eodice. 2005. Roots entwined: Growing a sustainable collaboration. In *Centers for learning: Writing centers and libraries in collaboration*, ed. J. K. Elmborg and S. Hook, 42–60. Chicago: Association of College and Research Libraries.

Gladwell, M. 2010. The sure thing: The myth of the daredevil entrepreneur. *New Yorker*, January 18, 24–29.

Hensley, R. B. 2006. Ways of thinking: Doing research and being information literate. In *Student engagement and information literacy*, ed. C. Gibson, 55–67. Chicago: Association of College and Research Libraries, American Library Association.

Huwe, T. K. 2004. Building digital libraries: Being organic gives reference librarians the edge over computers. *Computers in Libraries* 24:39–41.

Iannuzzi, P. 1998. Faculty development and information literacy: Establishing campus partnerships. *Reference Services Review* 26:97–102, 116.

Mackey, T. P., and T. E. Jacobson. 2005. Information literacy: A collaborative endeavor. *College Teaching* 53:140–44.

Mounce, M. 2010. Working together: Academic librarians and faculty collaborating to improve students' information literacy skills: A literature review 2000–2009. *The Reference Librarian* 51:300–20.

Neal, J. G. 2001. The entrepreneurial imperative advancing from incremental to radical change in the academic library. *Portal: Libraries and the Academy* 1:1–13.

Preston, G. 1984. How will automation affect cataloging staff? *Technical Services Quarterly* 1:129–36.

Rader, H. B. 1999. Faculty-librarian collaboration in building the curriculum for the millennium: The U.S. experience. *IFLA Journal* 25:209–13.

Raspa, R., and D. Ward. 2000. *The collaborative imperative: Librarians and faculty working together in the information universe.* Chicago: Association of College and Research Libraries.

Ratteray, O. M. T. 2002. Information literacy in self-study and accreditation. *The Journal of Academic Librarianship* 28:368–75.

Rider, M. M. 1996. Developing new roles for paraprofessionals in cataloging. *Journal of Academic Librarianship* 22:26–32.

Shumaker, D. 2009. Who let the librarians out?: Embedded librarianship and the library manager. *Reference & User Services Quarterly* 48:239–42.

Shumaker, D., and M. Talley. 2010. Models of embedded librarianship: A research summary. *Information Outlook* 14:26–35.

Shumaker, D., and L. A. Tyler. 2007. Embedded library services: An initial inquiry into practices for their development, management, and delivery. Paper presented at the Special Libraries Association Annual Conference, Denver, CO. http://www.sla.org/pdfs/sla2007/ShumakerEmbeddedLibSvcs.pdf.

Thompson, G. B. 2002. Information literacy accreditation mandates: What they mean for faculty and librarians. *Library Trends* 51:218–41.

Tucker: The man and his dream. 2000. DVD. Directed by Francis Ford Coppola. Hollywood: Paramount.

Villette, M., and C. Vuillermot. 2009. *From predators to icons: Exposing the myth of the business hero.* Ithaca, NY: ILR Press.

Watts, M. W., ed. 2008. Information literacy: One key to education. Special issue, *New Directions for Teaching and Learning*, no. 114.

Wegner, L. S. 1996. Is it true what they say?: The library on a credit card. *Journal of Academic Librarianship* 22:51–52.

Library Staff Development: How Book Clubs Can Be More Effective (and Less Expensive) than Traditional Trainings

SARA D. SMITH and QUINN GALBRAITH
Harold B. Lee Library, Brigham Young University, Provo, Utah, USA

Employee book clubs are simple, inexpensive tools for professional development that may be more effective than traditional training methods. Library staff at Brigham Young University participated in professional development book clubs, and they reported that they found these trainings to be more enjoyable than classroom-style trainings and more effective in helping them understand, retain, and apply the principles learned. This article will discuss the success of these book clubs and suggest ways that other libraries can implement cost-effective book clubs to develop professional and leadership skills.

INTRODUCTION

During times of financial strain and budget cuts, training budgets are usually the first to go. In light of reduced budgets and high training costs, libraries have been looking for less expensive and more effective ways to train and develop employees. The Harold B. Lee Library (HBLL) of Brigham Young University (BYU) found that employee book clubs are simple, inexpensive tools for professional and leadership development, and that they are perhaps more effective than traditional training methods.

Book clubs are not generally associated with professional development; the term often brings to mind images of friends eating cookies and discussing popular novels in living rooms, bookstores, or public libraries. But successful book clubs can create open, informal conversations that facilitate learning and development. As of late 2010, HBLL has been using book clubs to help library staff and faculty develop leadership and managerial skills for about one year. On surveys completed after participating in the book club, staff and faculty indicated that they prefer book clubs to traditional training methods, and that they can better retain and apply the material.

To demonstrate how and why book clubs are valuable training tools, the authors will explore survey results from HBLL's book clubs as well as research on how book clubs can effectively facilitate adult learning. Because book clubs are inexpensive, simple, and effective, we suggest that libraries utilize them for cost-effective training and professional development.

BOOK CLUBS AS ADULT EDUCATION AND EMPLOYEE DEVELOPMENT

Book clubs groups have been growing in popularity over the past few decades. Hartley and Turvey estimated in 2001 that there were about 500,000 book clubs in the United States, some held in living rooms, libraries, schools, bookstores, and even over the Internet. The number of both informal and institution-sponsored book groups has undoubtedly grown since then. "The idea isn't new—people have always read in groups—but [book clubs] are becoming increasingly popular . . . they have now earned their place on the cultural map" (Hartley and Turvey 2001, vii). Kerka suggested that the popularity of book clubs stems from the fact that "book groups fulfill the need for community and continuity in a constantly changing environment" (1996, 89).

Libraries and librarians are no strangers to book clubs—book clubs and reading groups have been used in public libraries for years. Bachman, Brown, and Whaley wrote that in 1997, the Madison Public Library in Wisconsin noticed that since fewer people were checking out books, they would introduce book discussion groups to "encourage patrons to go back to the older titles on the shelves, to revisit the classics, and perhaps most importantly to strengthen their sense of community" (2000, 13). These authors also noted that book clubs can help public libraries stay relevant to patrons in a technological age; "as libraries rely more and more on sophisticated technology, they give members a sense of community with a human touch" (13). Hoffert describes the creative approaches that several public libraries in the United States have been taking to implement book clubs: "librarians nationwide are successfully restructuring chitchat about beloved classics or recent bestsellers to deliver a richer and more vibrant experience for everyone" (2006, 37). Fajardo suggested that library-initiated reading groups could extend from public to academic libraries. She described a popular reading book club for students and faculty sponsored by the library at St. Catherine

University in Minnesota. The purpose of this book club was to "draw the community into the library, promote the library's image, and encourage lifelong learning and reading" (2010, 65). This book club usually drew many participants each semester and was relatively inexpensive.

Several researchers in the field of education, most notably Bauman (1994), have suggested that informal book groups can be effective and inexpensive methods of adult learning. Bauman wrote that "informal book groups are an important and often overlooked component of adult and continuing education," and that "the effectiveness and quality of book groups ... needs to be studied, specifically within the context of the needs and expectations of the participants" (38–39). Other researchers have looked at the effectiveness of book groups in motivating students to read and discuss literature, but not many have written about book clubs as methods of adult education.

Bauman observed eight book clubs attended monthly by adults and found that their discussions "consistently supported the value of informal, group-directed adult learning" (1994, 33). Bauman suggested that adults generally dislike formal, externally controlled education programs. However, in informal book groups, "without the pressures of degree-oriented coursework or the costs and short duration of a continuing education course, members were free to just learn" (36). Bauman observed that successful book clubs have a diverse membership, a variety in readings, semiformal ground rules determined by the group, and maintain an informal context. He also suggested that adult educators "need to think about independent learning, whether it is self-directed or group-directed" and consider informal learning groups in the facilitation of adult learning (39). Beyond the effectiveness of these methods, Bauman notes another "obvious incentive" to using book groups for adult education: "Informal designs can be simple and inexpensive ... [they have] no costs beyond the time to participate and the occasional expense of books or articles being discussed" (37).

Kerka notes that "talk is one of the ways through which human beings make meaning" (1996, 83), and that book club participants can transform collective and individual experiences into meaning or understanding through discussion. Like Bauman, she notes the importance of diversity in membership and informality in structure. In learning communities such as book groups, learners form mini-cultures that are "determined by the group's subconscious belief system, values, and attitudes about the dominant culture." (85) This shared culture creates a group cohesiveness, which "enables groups to operate smoothly and solidifies the atmosphere in which learning can take place" (85).

Bauman, Kerka, and others attributed the success of book clubs to the fact that they are not like school, where instruction and class interaction are formal and structured. Instead, the casual atmosphere fosters equality in discussion and turn-taking, as well as in the use of personal knowledge and experience. Addington notes that in adult book clubs, there is a "spirit of cooperation, collaboration, and personal sharing often absent in traditional classroom discussions" (2001, 216). Smith (1996) compared the discourse in adult book clubs to high school discussions of literature. He noted that the biggest difference between the two was the number of times that adults used their own lives and experiences as evidence. Merriam notes that the use of personal experience as a source of learning is an important characteristic of andragogy, a theory developed by Knowles in the late 1960s and 1970s to describe how adults learn differently than children. Book clubs give adult learners a forum in which to draw on and learn from their "reservoir of life experiences" (Merriam 2001, 5).

Smith noted that in traditional classroom settings, teachers orchestrate discussions by establishing rules, asking questions, and evaluating answers. Learners respond more to the teacher than to each other in discussions; for example, after each student takes a turn speaking, he or she returns the floor to the teacher instead of to another student. When teachers reveal their opinions on an issue, it "signals that the discussion of the issue is over; after all, they've given the 'right' answer" (184). However, Smith noted that the book club participants regularly responded directly to one another and equally shared the floor. The equal turn-taking demonstrated in book groups allows participants to explore the issue together and construct knowledge based on the experiences and opinions of each group member. Smith also noted that turn-taking allows group members to "work together to make a single point" (184) and actively engage in learning. Swanson analyzed the conversations of three adult book clubs and noted that participants "spoke for a slightly longer time than is common in classrooms," and as the discussion continued, they "spoke for increasingly longer periods of time" (1).

According to Bauman, book clubs can be classified as methods of "group-directed, informal learning" (1994, 37). He also said that book clubs fit the definition of self-directed learning in that they are a technique for self education and provide a forum for individuals to change their "value frameworks, moral codes, and cultural constructs" (37). In the clubs he observed, "group members were pursuing complex and personal goals that coincided with and reinforced the learning needs of other group members ... they were developing their ability to reflect and think critically, not only on the readings but on their own approach to group participation" (34). Book clubs are indeed an example of self-directed, or as Bauman suggests, group-directed learning, and they also are an opportunity for adults to develop and learn from engaging conversations. Swanson (1993) found that adult learners "benefit from a chance to develop group discussions and relationships surrounding texts, and they may benefit from and enjoy a chance to explore their own and each other's ideas without direction" (1).

In addition to self-directed learning, another model of adult education is relevant to a discussion of the effectiveness of book clubs: the model of conversational learning, which argues that conversation enables adults to construct meaning from their own and each other's experiences. It is "a process whereby learners construct new meaning and transform their collective experiences into knowledge through their conversations" (Baker, Jensen, and Kolb 2005, 412). Because conversation allows adults to "face situations that are beyond their current capacities to know as individuals," Kayes proposes conversational learning as an alternative to traditional professional development methods (2002, 203).

In conversational learning in the workplace, knowledge is not limited solely to the trainer or educator; conversation transforms individual experiences into group knowledge. The role of the workplace trainer is to create space for conversation and encourage employees to contribute. Conversational learning "promises to enhance the learning experiences of organizational members" as thinking shifts from "individual learning to group learning" (Kayes 2002, 204). Book clubs can provide a forum for learning through conversations that can "catalyze visions, innovations for new development, and learning" (Baker, Jensen, and Kolb 2002, 4). They move beyond traditional methods of employee education to provide an environment for employees to cultivate and practice leadership skills. Traditional "lecture methods" of employee education are ineffective because they "locate the source of 'knowledge' in one individual, the lecturer," and in doing so, the "skills and experiences which participants brought with them into the classroom" are ignored (Doyle 1992, 24). However, in book clubs, employees learn from each other and from their own experiences "by combining individual strengths in personality and areas of knowledge ... [as] the group becomes smarter and more effective than the sum of the individuals" (Jacobsohn 1994, 64).

In discussing possible applications for research demonstrating the effectiveness of book clubs as adult education, Kerka suggests that adult educators "serve as brokers for the formation of learning networks" and "form book groups as a staff development method for themselves and for other organizations" (1996, 89). Several organizations and industries have capitalized on the popularity of informal, "living-room" book clubs by using them as a method for training and development. Most notably, book groups have been used by teachers as a resource for change and professional development. Peer book groups have been used to train new teachers (Dengler, Lassonde, and Sterns 2005; Kooy 2006) and to introduce literature that could be used in the classroom. Teacher book groups have read academic and professional literature and shared or evaluated various classroom methods (Flood and Lapp 1994; Pelletier 1993; Selway 2003). Smit (2003), Raphael et al. (2001), and Hoerr (2009) described the implementation of school- and district-wide changes based on ideas generated in faculty book groups. Other professions have used book groups for employee development, including nurses (Greenawald 2008; Steffen 2006), HR professionals (Bonner and Tarner 1999), contractors (Raftery 2007), credit unions (Brown 2007), and insurance companies (Dolezalek 2002). It is likely that other industries and companies have successfully used this method as well.

BOOK CLUBS AT HBLL

HBLL has also extended the use of book clubs to a method of professional and employee development in an academic library. Unlike popular "living-room" book clubs in which the same group of people meets regularly to discuss different books, HBLL started a new group for each book and has so far sponsored three staff book clubs. Participation in each group was voluntary and open to all employees, both staff and faculty, from any department. Participants for each group were recruited with an e-mail that the human resource manager sent out to all employees. One group read and discussed a book about Web design, while the other two read books that focused on managerial and leadership skills. After completing the book club, participants were surveyed about their experiences. Library leaders were initially hesitant to sponsor these book clubs because they were not sure if the program would be productive; thus, the surveys were administered to provide feedback. The results were surprisingly positive; they showed that library staff and faculty enjoyed the training, felt that they were better able to retain and internalize the principles, and preferred book clubs to traditional trainings.

Don't Make Me Think. The first group, composed of twenty-six staff and faculty, read Krug's *Don't Make Me Think,* which discusses Web design and usability. This group was organized and implemented by a library staff member who wanted to help other employees improve technology skills. The postsurvey indicated that the book club was effective in helping participants retain, internalize, and use the information presented in the book, and that participants desired to participate again. Participants were asked to rate the usefulness of the book club on a scale of one to ten (ten being the most useful), and the average rating was 8.5. Group members rated the book club's ability to help them internalize the principles on a scale of one to ten at an average of 8.2. Participants also commented on the value of the discussions: "This was much better than just reading it, because it allowed for internalization and discussion. We could debate many of the points stated in the book." Another wrote, "Reading it as a group allowed for discussion, not only of the principles being discussed, but of their application to the work being done in the library and in our departments." Ninety-six percent of participants indicated that they would participate in another book club. One even wrote, "I hope the book club can cover a wide set of topics and help us learn how to be more valuable contributors to the library."

Death by Meeting. Because of the success of the first group, HBLL created a second book club to focus on managerial and leadership skills. This group was formed by the human resource manager and read Lencioni's *Death by Meeting,* which discusses the effective use of meetings in an organization. Book club participants were split into two smaller groups that met separately, and members of both clubs were surveyed six months after the book club ended. Even with the time gap, the survey showed that participants were using principles from the training. On a scale of one to five, 54 percent rated the usefulness of the book club at four, and 15 percent rated it at five. Ninety-two percent reported that they were able to apply a principle discussed in the book club to their work. Even six months after finishing the book, participants referred to ideas and terms from the book in their comments and were able to list specific changes they made as a result of the book club. Even employees who do not hold leadership positions found the club useful: "I don't conduct meetings," wrote one participant, "but I am no longer afraid to bring up topics or ask questions that might spur a little contentious discussion."

The survey results also suggest that staff and faculty prefer book clubs to traditional classroom-style trainings, especially when it comes to leadership and managerial skills. Participants were asked to rate book club trainings and traditional trainings on a scale of one to five in four categories: enjoyment, participation, ability to understand/internalize the principles, and ability to retain the principles discussed. Participants rated the book club higher by almost one point in every category (See Table 1). The biggest gaps were in enjoyment and in participation. Participants were also asked to indicate which training format they would prefer for learning managerial, supervisory, or leadership principles. Again, the book club was the favorite; 92 percent preferred this format over classroom-style trainings. Of course, the HBLL staff and faculty surveyed represent a small sample of library employees, and these employees volunteered to participate in the book club perhaps because they expected to enjoy the experience. Even so, we believe that these results suggest that employee book clubs are more effective and enjoyable tools for professional development.

TABLE 1 *Death by Meeting* Survey Results: Book Clubs vs. Traditional Trainings

Category	Traditional trainings	Book club trainings
Enjoyment of the training	3.1	4.2
Participation in the training	3.0	4.3
Ability to understand and internalize the principles	3.6	4.2
Retention of the principles	3.0	4.0

Note. Average rating on a 1 to 5 scale, 5 being the highest.

TABLE 2 *Emotional Intelligence* Survey Results: Book Clubs vs. Traditional Trainings

Category	Traditional trainings	Book club trainings
Enjoyment of the training	3.1	4.0
Participation in the training	2.6	4.1
Ability to understand and internalize the principles	3.3	4.1
Retention of the principles	2.8	3.6

Note. Average rating on a 1 to 5 scale, 5 being the highest.

Emotional Intelligence. Survey results from the third book club echoed results from the second. This group read *Emotional Intelligence* by Goleman. This book was suggested by a group of instruction and education librarians who met regularly to discuss journal articles published in their field. As with the other two book clubs, HBLL advertised this group by sending e-mails to invite library employees to participate. The response to these e-mails showed the increasing popularity of the book clubs—about 25 percent of our full-time employees responded with interest. Again, two smaller book clubs were created from this group. The first group was comprised of members of HBLL's journal club, who met together regularly before participating in the book club to discuss current literature about library instruction. The second group was comprised of staff and faculty from various departments.

Both groups were surveyed separately, but results were similar: The first group rated the usefulness of the book club (on a one to five scale) at an average of 3.7, and the second group rated it at 3.6. Seventy-one percent of participants in both groups reported to have applied a principle from *Emotional Intelligence* to their work, and all participants reported that they prefer book clubs over traditional trainings. As with the *Death by Meeting* group, the survey asked group members to compare book clubs and classroom-style trainings—and, again, book clubs were rated higher in every category (See Table 2).

Some participants indicated both on the survey and in the book club discussions that they did not enjoy reading *Emotional Intelligence*—the book was described in comments as "labored," "redundant," "a bit hard to slog through," and even "mind-bogglingly boring." These reactions make the positive survey results even more significant: while some staff and faculty did not like reading the book, they did enjoy the book club.

CREATING CONVERSATION: CHARACTERISTICS OF EFFECTIVE BOOK CLUBS

As discussed, several researchers have noted key factors that make book clubs effective. These factors include: membership, readings, semiformal ground rules, and informal context (Bauman 1994); people, structure, and culture (Kerka 1996); social aspect, equality among club members, and a spirit of cooperation (Smith 1996); and cooperation, collaboration, and personal sharing (Addington 2001). There are clearly some similarities and overlap among these principles. Drawing on this research and our own experience, we suggest three characteristics of successful, conversation-starting book clubs that encompass these factors. These characteristics are group direction, diverse membership, and informal atmosphere. By integrating these attributes, libraries can create successful employee book clubs that lead to effective learning.

Group Direction

In a self-directed learning model, individual learners determine how and what they learn by setting their own learning objectives. As Bauman noted, book clubs encourage self-directed learning—or rather, group-directed learning—because group members, individually and collectively, become responsible for their own learning by establishing a group format, selecting readings and discussion topics, and participating in the conversation. As club members work together, groups develop their own norms and their "own spirit, soul, and style" (Kerka 1996, 84). Obviously, the determination of rules, format, and readings will be more flexible in "living-room" book clubs than in the workplace, but HBLL was still able to incorporate flexibility and accommodate the needs of group members. The book used in each of HBLL's book clubs was selected based on suggestions from staff members—and the idea for the book club itself originated from a library employee. The human resource manager planned and scheduled the discussions, but participants were invited to voice their interests and preferences.

Book club members are their own and each other's teachers. In HBLL's *Emotional Intelligence* book club, two different facilitators volunteered to lead each discussion. The facilitators rotated each meeting, which ensured that new perspectives were heard and that the club was led by the group and not by one person. One participant in this group commented that having "rotating facilitators was helpful in keeping everyone engaged." Facilitation itself is a development tool: for the facilitators, the book club became a forum to not only learn but also practice leadership skills, which would not be possible through traditional trainings.

Diversity

Several researchers noted the importance of diversity in book clubs. Smith observed that a book club's informal context "gave members a chance to learn about more than the personal experiences of their colleagues"—

members also were able to "gain insights into their friends" and their values and views (1996, 183). This opportunity for insight and understanding is enhanced by diversity in membership, which guarantees a wide range of experiences. Diversity can exist not only in race, gender, age, etc., but also in background, opinion, and thought: "a variety of opinions and experiences lend themselves to discussion and exploration of new ideas. Given that conversation is the primary form of exchange, the backgrounds and experiences of members often becomes the basis for reflection and understanding" (Bauman 1994, 34). Learning through conversation requires diversity in thought and experience—otherwise, participants cannot learn as effectively from the group. Because of this, library book clubs should be comprised of a diverse membership. This does not pose a huge challenge, because libraries are inherently diverse when it comes to employee background, interests, and experience. HBLL book club members came from all over the library, including cataloging, information technology, administration, and various subject areas. Both library staff and faculty participated in the book clubs, and this led to interesting, broad conversations that reflected many viewpoints.

Informal Atmosphere

As evident in the literature, particularly the study comparing book club discourse to classroom discussions conducted by Smith, book clubs are not as structured and formal as classroom environments. Participants in HBLL's book clubs appreciated the opportunity to discuss the books' concepts in small groups. As discussed, staff and faculty who participated in the *Death by Meeting* and *Emotional Intelligence* groups rated book club trainings significantly higher than classroom-style trainings in their ability to participate and share ideas. A participant in the *Emotional Intelligence* group commented, "I liked having a small group for discussions; I felt comfortable about sharing my ideas"; another said, "It was interesting to read on my own and form opinions and then to hear how other people interpret the same information. Sometimes my views were changed or enhanced because of the discussion." The informality of small group discussions book clubs allows participants to talk openly and freely and reach conclusions they would not have discovered alone.

Book clubs are inherently informal, and HBLL reinforced this by using volunteer facilitators, group-generated questions and ideas, and by providing casual snacks at book club meetings. The physical environment can also contribute to a casual atmosphere. The "physical arrangement of seating in a circle enhances the sense of equal status among members, creating a comfortable, safe atmosphere in which participants feel free to share ideas, feelings, and disagreement" (Kerka 1996, 85). HBLL held its book clubs in conference rooms, where participants, including the facilitators, sat in a circle around a table. An informal physical environment can help participants feel comfortable interacting directly with group members as they participate in the conversation.

REDUCING TRAINING COST

There are many reasons that account for the effectiveness of this format in professional development—not the least of which is cost. HBLL traditionally uses seminars, Webinars, and other lecture or classroom-style trainings, which can be costly. Webinars usually cost between $100 and $300, but generally have low turn-outs—HBLL sometimes only has about five to ten people show up. Bringing in outside trainers or lecturers can be even more expensive, sometimes costing between $2,000 and $4,000. In comparison, book clubs are relatively inexpensive. For example, HBLL bought copies of *Emotional Intelligence* online at a group discount for $11 each. There was no need for a paid trainer or facilitators—the participants became the trainers, both for themselves and for each other.

However, the time it takes to read the books was a possible concern. HBLL did not indicate to employees whether they should read the books on or off the clock. On both the *Death by Meeting* and *Emotional Intelligence* surveys, participants were asked how much time they spent reading at work. Participants in both groups indicated that on average they spent equal time reading the book at work and at home. Even without direction, employees chose on their own to read both at home and at work.

CONCLUSION: IMPLEMENTING BOOK CLUBS AT YOUR LIBRARY

Because book clubs are simple and inexpensive, they can be used in any library of any size. The model used by HBLL could easily be used or adjusted to meet the needs of each library. Based on our experience, we offer the following suggestions for implementing book clubs for library staff:

- Use surveys. Informal surveys given before and/or after the book club can evaluate the success of the club and gauge the interest of library staff and faculty in participating in future book clubs. Surveys can also provide suggestions for improvement.
- Choose business or leadership books that are applicable to all library employees. This also ensures that all participants, no matter where they work in the library, can engage in the conversation and develop leadership or managerial skills, and that participants have the opportunity to read books outside of their professional reading.
- Research the book before assigning it to the book club. As discussed, some HBLL participants did not enjoy reading *Emotional Intelligence*. HBLL

leadership was not familiar with this book before the book club read it; thus, in the future, we plan to examine book suggestions by reading reviews and portions of the book.

- Make participation voluntary, and encourage employees in all library departments to participate. This ensures diversity and lively, engaged conversations.

After experimenting with book clubs as a way to train and develop library employees, HBLL found that this method is less expensive than traditional classroom-style trainings, and that employees prefer this method to traditional trainings. Staff and faculty who participated in HBLL's book clubs reported that they not only found this method more enjoyable than traditional methods, but that it was also more effective in helping them understand, retain, and apply the principles discussed. After completing the *Emotional Intelligence* book club, one participant wrote, "I find it helpful to discuss ideas with other people in a book club format rather than just having a lecture. I have found it helps in my retention and ability to apply principles." We suggest that other academic libraries experiment with this simple, effective, and inexpensive tool. By using book clubs, libraries can significantly reduce training costs, and, at the same time, create conversations that help library staff develop professional, managerial, and leadership skills.

REFERENCES

Addington, A. H. 2001. Talking about literature in university book club and seminar settings. *Research in the Teaching of English* 36:212–48.

Bachman, P., A. Brown, and I. Whaley. 2000. Henrico Library patrons connect with books. *Virginia Libraries* 46:13–16.

Baker, A. C., P. J. Jensen, and D. A. Kolb. 2002. Learning and conversation. In *Conversational learning: An experiential approach to knowledge creation*, eds. A. Baker, P. Jensen, and D. Kolb, 1–13. New York: Quorum Books.

Baker, A. C., P. J. Jensen, and D. A. Kolb. 2005. Conversation as experiential learning. *Management Learning* 36:411–27.

Bauman, P. 1994. Book groups: Informal and innovative adult learning. *Journal of Adult Education* 22:31–41.

Bonner, D., and L. Tarner. 1999. Once upon an HRD book club. *Training and Development* 53:45–51.

Brown, L. S. 2007. Lessons learned: Leadership team book club. *Credit Union Management* 30:12.

Dengler, K., C. Lassonde, and K. Sterns. 2005. What are you reading in book groups? Developing reading lives in teacher candidates. *Action in Teacher Education* 27:43–53.

Dolezalek H. 2002. Reading Circle. *Training* 39:20.

Doyle, M. 1992. Challenges in trade union education: A case for active learning. *Labour Education* 87:24–27.

Fajardo, A. 2010. Book clubs: Not just for public libraries. *College & Undergraduate Libraries* 17:65–69.

Flood, J., and D. Lapp. 1994. Teacher book clubs: Establishing literature discussion groups for Teachers. *The Reading Teacher* 47:274–76.

Goleman, D. 2006. *Emotional intelligence.* New York: Bantam.

Greenawald, D. 2008. School nurse book clubs: An innovative strategy of lifelong learning. *Journal of School Nursing* 24:61–65.

Hartley, J., and S. Tuvey. 2001. *Reading groups.* New York: Oxford University Press.

Hoerr, T. R. 2009. How book groups bring change. *Educational Leadership* 66:80–82.

Hoffert, B. 2006. The book club exploded. *Library Journal*, August 7, 34–37.

Jacobsohn, R. W. 1994. *The reading group handbook.* New York: Hyperion.

Kayes, C. D. 2002. Conversational learning in organization and human resource developments. In *Conversational learning: An experiential approach to knowledge creation*, ed. A. Baker, P. Jensen, and D. Kolb, 193–205. New York: Quorum Book.

Kerka, S. 1996. Book groups: Communities of learners. *New Directions for Adult and Continuing Education* 71:81–90.

Kooy, M. 2006. The telling stories of novice teachers: Constructing teacher knowledge in book clubs. *Teaching & Teacher Education* 22:661–74.

Krug, S. 2005. *Don't make me think.* Berkley: New Riders Publishing.

Lencioni, P. 2004. *Death by meeting.* San Francisco: Jossey-Bass.

Merriam, S. B. 2001. Andragogy and self-directed learning: Pillars of adult learning theory. *New Directions for Adult and Continuing Education* 89:3–13.

Pelletier, C. M. 1993. Professional development through a teacher book club. Paper presented at the annual meeting of the American Education Research Association, Atlanta, GA.

Raftery, D. 2007. Starting down the 7 measures path. *Associations Now* 3:14–15.

Raphael T. E., S. FlorioRuane, M. J. Kehus, M. George, N. L. Hasty, and K. Highfield. 2001. Thinking for ourselves: Literacy learning in a diverse teacher inquiry network. *The Reading Teacher* 54:596–607.

Selway, L. G. 2003. Leading a professional book club: Staff development to build understanding and grapple with difficult issues. Paper presented at the annual meeting of the American Research Association, Chicago, IL.

Smit G. 2003. To infuse new thinking, Try book discussions. *School Administrator* 58:34.

Smith, M. W. 1996. Conversations about literature outside classrooms: How adults talk about books in their book clubs. *Journal of Adolescent and Adult Literacy* 40:164–240.

Steffen, L. 2006. Forming a book club for nurses. *Creative Nursing* 12:12.

Swanson, Ann. 1993. Adult book club discussions: Response as a key. Paper presented at the annual meeting of the National Reading Conference, Charleston, SC.

The NYU Survey Service: Promoting Value in Undergraduate Education

JASON B. PHILLIPS, SAMANTHA A. GUSS, and DAVID M. McGARRY
New York University, New York, New York, USA

New York University's (NYU) Data Service Studio has recently launched the NYU Survey Service, whose ultimate aim is to support the development and administration of surveys of all types. For the Web-based component, the service utilizes a product called Qualtrics, which allows university affiliates to develop and administer Web-based surveys. This article describes the process by which NYU came to offer the service during a time when concerns abound about the ability of libraries to support and expand offerings while still meeting institutional imperatives such as robust data services. While many considerations went into the evaluation and ultimate conclusion to pilot the service, this article considers those most related to library collaborations, undergraduate instruction, data and information literacy, learning and research, and application administration and support.

Current economic conditions notwithstanding, library collections and services must still support sound teaching and learning. The academy's needs and activities are evolving and this change requires modified or new services from libraries. It is within this context that New York University Libraries' Data Service Studio (DSS) identified a significant opportunity to better support numeric and geospatial research. The solution required a more expansive, less insulated, approach to the selection of the online component for our newly introduced NYU Survey Service. And the value of the service to research and learning was among the prominent underpinnings of our exploration of a resolution.

As the breadth of electronic resources and tools available for use continue to proliferate and evolve, user expectations will remain high regardless of the library's fiscal condition. One expectation is that the library will support the learning activities of the university's undergraduate students, which increasingly means support of original research by undergraduates. The ability to support survey research methodologies in a manner that is rigorous and ethical is fundamental to that expectation. And it was that necessity that prompted DSS staff to pursue partnerships and input that might not have been considered during the evaluation of an electronic tool in the past. However, such a process may prove increasingly necessary in the "new normal." Save for the approach outlined below, the DSS would have likely been unable to offer truly robust support for the provision of online surveys by NYU affiliates. This article describes the causes and rationale for the development of the survey service, making special reference to how prevailing trends and attitudes about undergraduate education and its value drove the processes from problem identification to implementation. The selection process described here led to the selection and introduction of the Qualtrics Web survey tool.

SUPPORTING DATA DRIVEN RESEARCH IN LIBRARIES

Selecting, acquiring, and supporting a robust university-wide Web survey tool marks an important step in the evolution of NYU's DSS. The DSS, which opened in fall 2008, brings together statistical computing and library data services in a physical location in NYU's Bobst Library with a central mission of supporting members of the NYU community in their work at all stages of the research life cycle (Green and Gutmann 2007) of numeric and spatial data. By providing a tool for the creation of data, the DSS is effectively supporting a key piece of that life cycle.

The NYU Data Service Studio, a joint venture of Information Technology Services (hereafter, ITS) and the Division of Libraries, is designed to provide support for numeric and spatial data-oriented research projects. DSS services, which are continually evolving, include (1) a dedicated and centrally located lab equipped with the hardware and software to conduct quantitative, qualitative, and geographical research analysis; (2) statistical consultation and instruction; (3) tutorials and training materials on research software and methods; and (4) support for the acquisition and use of numeric and spatial data sets among other services. The full-time DSS staff is currently comprised of two statisticians, two librarians, two IT professionals, and a geographer.

Graduate students from five NYU schools and six unique degree programs are also employed and consult based upon their high-level knowledge of the various statistical and mapping software packages supported by the DSS. For a visual representation of this model, see McGarry and Guss (2010). (Also see the DSS Website at http://nyu.libguides.com/dataservicestudio.)

Although the DSS has only existed for two years, ITS and the Libraries had independently and separately supported aspects of quantitative research and numeric data activities for years. Both units provided access to statistical software packages. The statisticians and faculty technology specialists in ITS supported statistical computing in a variety of ways: helping users navigate statistical software packages, providing research design consultations, and helping users find data from sources like the United States Census Bureau and the Inter-University Consortium for Political and Social Research (ICPSR). Meanwhile, librarians helped users find and access information, often in the form of numeric data, in the context of comprehensive literature searches. The library also harbored expertise in sophisticated preservation and description of resources and discovery environments and techniques. It was because of these complimentary skill sets that these two groups merged, creating the foundation for the Data Service Studio. One of the things that became clear in planning for the DSS was the importance of providing users with a single place in which they could address all of their data needs.

The DSS's main goal is to support the NYU community at *all stages* of the digital life cycle of numeric and spatial data by "provid[ing] integrated support for NYU faculty and students in finding, accessing, understanding, manipulating, sharing and preserving the raw materials of research for multiple disciplines across the university" (NYU Data Services Working Group 2007). In this list of objectives, we can find much of the same language of the Digital Curation Centre's Curation Lifecycle—the sequential actions Create or Receive; Appraise & Select; Ingest; Preservation Action; Store; Access, Use, & Reuse; and Transform—and the actions that should occur throughout the lifecycle: Description and Representation Information, Preservation Planning, Community Watch and Participation, and Curate and Preserve (Digital Curation Centre 2010).

While the Data Service Studio has been skillfully supporting pieces of this life cycle since its inception, especially the components titled "Access, Use, & Reuse," "Transform," and "Community Watch and Participation," others are still in planning or development stages. We are continuing to build our expertise in the various preservation actions and piloting several data repository projects as we determine our best path toward supporting the preservation of numeric and spatial data. Regardless of whether full-scale digital preservation services will be provided locally by the DSS or whether we instead serve as facilitator between researchers and already established archives, we can still actively build services across the spectrum, including support for those collecting or creating data. The NYU Survey Service

(Qualtrics) allows us to add "Create" to our list of supported life cycle actions. Providing a Web-based survey tool that has been carefully vetted to meet the high standards of our researchers and to serve as a teaching tool for the instructors of budding undergraduate data creators moves us considerably closer to our goal of full life cycle support. Certainly NYU is not the only institution of higher education that has acted to add data services to its library and information technology offerings; in fact many institutions already have or certainly will need data services (Aldrich and Stefanelli 2006), and Internet-based Web survey tools will be an increasingly important part of the array of services offered (Farrell and Petersen 2010).

QUANTITATIVE LITERACY AND ORIGINAL RESEARCH BY UNDERGRADUATES

By acquiring a university-wide license for a Web survey tool, the Data Service Studio is not only supporting faculty, administrative, and institutional research, but also the learning and research needs of undergraduates and providing them with important transferable skills. Access to rigorous research tools is crucial considering the increased emphasis on quantitative literacy, quantitative reasoning, and original research skills in recent years (Madison and Steen 2008; Steen 2004).

An important trend is the push to strengthen quantitative literacy skills across the undergraduate curriculum, commonly described as the quantitative literacy, or QL, "movement." McClure and Sircar (2008, 369), writing particularly about business education, argue that "quantitative methods can and should be applied to a wide array of decision-making scenarios and that all business students should have an adequate level of quantitative literacy to make calculated decisions in the increasingly complex, information-oriented, knowledge-based world"—a statement that can apply to students across many, if not all, disciplines. Informed participation in society depends not only on traditional notions of literacy—the ability to interpret information—but increasingly the ability to comprehend and interpret information represented numerically or derived from quantitative methods. Schield (2004, 6) argues that it will be "difficult to be considered information literate in the 21st century without being statistically literate," and others have argued that undergraduates in the United States are already falling behind in attaining these skills (McClure and Sircar, for instance).

The literature logically identifies statistics and mathematics educators as key figures, but also emphasizes that QL is widely relevant and more effectively achieved when "explicitly label[ed], model[ed], and reinforce[d] repeatedly in multiple contexts" (Jordan and Haines 2006). A quantitative-reasoning-across-the-curriculum (QRAC) approach has been championed for years by leaders in the QL movement (Cozzens 2003). The QRAC approach, "reflecting the well-established writing-across-the-curriculum model, asks instructors in all disciplines to incorporate explanations of quantitative reasoning and quantitative problem solving in their teaching" (Jordan and Haines 2006). There are countless examples of courses, faculty members, and entire departments that have prioritized incorporation of QL principles in disciplines like business, sociology, and social justice, but there is also a role for the library, and particularly for library data services centers. Schield (2004, 9) argues that librarians, who are generalists already involved in teaching critical thinking and information literacy, are "eminently qualified to teach students . . . how to become statistically literate and how to become data literate."

Another important trend is the increased emphasis on original research conducted by undergraduates, and this phenomenon has been well-chronicled in the library and information science and education literature (Hunter, Laursen, and Seymour 2006). The opportunity for rewards to students and society from undergraduates who are trained to efficiently produce and interpret data can be significant (Card et al. 2003; Higgins 1999). Students who emerge from undergraduate programs with these skills offer benefits to society and will have an advantage in the knowledge-driven economy's difficult job market.

Original research has been prescribed as a mode of pedagogy in large introductory courses in the social sciences (Atkinson, Czaja, and Brewster 2006) as a method of teaching statistics to nonmajors (MacDougall 2008), and naturally as part of research methods courses for undergraduates in a variety of disciplines including sociology, business, and political science, among others (Doyle and Mezzell 2007; Shostak et al. 2010; Vandiver and Walsh 2010).

In addition to these in-class reasons that students are conducting original research, many liberal arts colleges require a thesis or capstone project, while many larger research universities, including New York University, have honors programs for undergraduates that culminate in a senior thesis derived from original research. Providing full support for these pedagogical and curricular endeavors should mean instruction or tutoring in appropriate methods as well as institutional support for the necessary tools. Survey research in particular spans a wide range of disciplines, and these surveys are often created and administered via the Web—necessitating the availability of a Web-based survey tool.

ECONOMIC CONSOLIDATION ARGUMENTS

In our initial research, we discovered that other units on campus, as well as countless individuals, were already paying to use Web survey tools. As a result, we considered the purchase of a survey tool with an eye toward streamlining the approach while simultaneously expanding campus capabilities. The Web-based survey tool provided by Qualtrics Inc. was already being used by at least one school at New York University, but, of course, most NYU affiliates did not have access to that product. Several schools and administrative departments had purchased limited licenses to other survey products (for instance, Snap Surveys), while others shared a single Survey Monkey (or other) account. Beyond these known expenditures, we knew from experience that countless faculty members, graduate students, and undergraduate students were purchasing individual accounts to tools such as Survey Monkey.

While the DSS officially provided support for Survey Monkey and maintained access to several accounts for our own instructional purposes, we had previously been unable to provide individual, secure accounts to our users. In order to gain access to a tool where surveys could be administered confidentially, users were counseled to acquire—and pay for—their own individual accounts.

The true cost savings of a university-wide license might be realized by allowing any affiliates or units to stop paying for other survey solutions on an *ad hoc* basis. ITS would pay the full licensing cost and could expect to recover up to 25 to 50 percent of the licensing cost from other university units by agreements with other units. The cost of support and outreach would be split between the Division of Libraries and ITS. A centralized solution would make support and administration more efficient and eliminate the cost burden from individuals, which would be especially significant for students. Qualtrics was selected because of its own merits, but it was certainly an added bonus that the other units that were already paying for Qualtrics (and uninterested in switching tools) could be incorporated into the university-wide price. We also reached out to units that might not necessarily contribute money but that might be interested in the rollout of such a product with the goal of increasing university-wide buy-in and recognition for the survey service. The interests of these units varied and included managerial and administrative reasons and even reasons related to the promotion of or compliance with standards of ethical research behavior. We worked to ensure that the needs or requirements of these units were met before we finalized the service. Additionally, a cost recovery model was defined such that any of these units could get a customized look and feel or "skin" in return for a contribution to the overall cost of the tool. Providing an enterprise solution for users at NYU allows the entire campus to leverage both the efficiencies and methodological advantages that come with the use of online surveys.

SELECTION PROCESS

In order to select and recommend a Web survey tool for purchase, the Data Service Studio team completed an evaluation that involved gathering information, characterizing the future service, defining requirements for a tool, identifying tools to evaluate, and evaluating each of the defined criteria.

The following steps represent the approach to selection and were employed roughly in the order below.

1. Gather community input to verify the demand and functional requirements for a survey service.
2. Research existing survey tools and service models at NYU and identify gaps and potential for improvements.
3. Summarize functional requirements and define administrative requirements for a survey service.
4. Identify potential tools and evaluate them based on stated functional and administrative requirements.
5. Define the Data Service Studio survey service model needed to accommodate the distribution and support of a centralized university-wide survey service.
6. Evaluate the cost effectiveness of a single centrally supported solution.
7. Make a recommendation based on information gathered during the evaluation process.

To learn about survey needs, we targeted several groups: known existing survey users at NYU, other survey tool providers at NYU that were previously known or discovered during this project, and personnel at peer institutions who either support or use surveys.

A Web survey was administered to Data Service Studio clients who were known have conducted survey research as well as to the members of a "Statistics" Listserv, a special interest list comprised of NYU faculty, staff, and students who voluntarily elected to receive information about the Data Service Studio. This survey generated thirty-one responses (eighteen faculty, seven staff, six students) from twelve schools and departments, and it yielded valuable insight from the community about desired features and tools already in use, while indicating a high level of interest in a new centralized solution. Contact was also made with several individuals across the NYU campus who were affiliated with departments expected to administer surveys (e.g., the Leonard N. Stern School of Business and various NYU administrative offices). Finally, a Web search was conducted to learn about survey services and solutions currently offered by NYU's peer institutions and to identify potential tools to evaluate.

Functional requirements were compiled using feedback from the survey of users and from the previous experience gathered by Data Service Studio staff from years of supporting Survey Monkey. Administrative requirements were also defined largely on this existing knowledge and experience, but also refined over the course of the evaluation. For instance, the definition of a "reasonable" price emerged only after several products had been evaluated. Additionally, DSS staff had a good idea of the type of service model that they could realistically employ, but details of this ideal model also surfaced only after an in-depth look at the tools and vendors themselves.

The final list of tools to be evaluated was compiled from the assessments of peer institutions and tools already supported and used on the NYU campus. Eight tools were evaluated. An initial investigation of each tool was conducted by contacting vendors and compiling information from vendor Websites. For tools that met initial administrative requirements, the evaluation team scheduled a demonstration that was conducted via Webinar. Trial accounts were obtained for several tools so that evaluators could get a first-hand sense of the tool and its features. Additionally, after Qualtrics emerged as the finalist, the evaluators contacted colleagues from another NYU unit and from a peer institution, both of whom were already supporting Qualtrics, to gather impressions. In addition to evaluating the stated requirements, interactions with the vendors also gave DSS staff a sense of how each vendor handled interactions with its customers and what each might be like to work with.

Although functional requirements were certainly important, administrative requirements were evaluated first. The evaluators acknowledged that even the most feature-rich tool would be eliminated if it did not meet critical administrative requirements—for example, if it were prohibitively expensive or required so much administrative overhead that the Data Service Studio could not realistically support it. For this reason, not all tools were fully evaluated, as many were necessarily eliminated from consideration based on clear inability to fulfill administrative requirements. Survey Monkey also was not evaluated via a demonstration because DSS staff evaluators had sufficient knowledge of its features from years of supporting it.

The fact that NYU chose Qualtrics as the underlying tool for this aspect of our online survey services reflects the confluence among Qualtrics, NYU's needs, resources, and the opinions of those charged with the evaluation of the several tools we appraised. The DSS selected Qualtrics based on the evaluation presented here, but this article is not meant to definitively recommend (or discourage) that other institutions select Qualtrics as their Web survey tool. Each institution will undoubtedly uncover different administrative and functional requirements based on their assessment of their own unique user communities and circumstances. Instead, this article is presented as a recommendation for how other institutions might go about determining these needs and requirements so that they can choose among survey tools with an eye toward greater efficiency and cost savings without sacrificing methodological robustness or ethical research.

ADMINISTRATIVE AND FUNCTIONAL REQUIREMENTS

Based upon the needs expressed by NYU users and available resources at hand, the NYU Survey Service Project team members defined the following list of five administrative requirements for potential survey solutions: (1) the tool must be available at a reasonable price for all current faculty, staff and students of NYU, and, ideally, the tool would offer a site-license option to ensure that the price would not be contingent upon the number of active users or respondents; (2) due to the limited number of in-house resources to run, maintain, and backup a server, the tool was also required to provide secure hosting; (3) similarly, limited staff time required the tool to offer a form of automated provisioning so that user accounts were automatically created, validated, and deleted according to NYU's registry system; (4) to ensure portability, the tool must be Web-based so that it can be accessed on any machine, Windows, Macintosh, Linux, etc., without additional software installation; and (5) the final administrative requirement was a method of collecting usage metrics of the tool so that the DSS can monitor current needs and project future user needs.

The survey of known survey users across NYU solidified a list of desired features for a Web survey tool. Heading the list was the need for an intuitive graphical user interface so that users from all backgrounds could use the tool with relative ease. Another component was a method for collaboration or sharing so that multiple users, or groups, could edit and view the same survey(s). Users also wanted a powerful mechanism for respondent management, one that allowed batch lists of respondents to be uploaded and contacted based on various conditional statements, for instance if they had, or had not, completed a survey. Other key elements included the ability to directly export raw data to SPSS's file format (.sav) with value labels attached, eliminating the cumbersome and unnecessary process of entering them manually; advanced randomization and logic capabilities; options for the viewing and analysis of results; plug-in capabilities for embedded video; integrated scripting options; templates for sample surveys and survey questions; and respondent-based metadata and foreign language support. There was also a demand for paper-based surveys, but given the hardware requirements (automatic feed scanners) and limited benefits in the academic setting—few functional features and only negligible advantages in survey response rate and quality (Fricker and Schonlau 2002, 347–58)—a paper-based option was deemed unnecessary and impractical for a large-scale service. Additionally, the DSS provides access to a feed scanner and the software package Remark OMR on an appointment basis to the few users who cannot use Web-based surveys for their research.

RECOMMENDATION

Table 1 represents the rubric used to evaluate each tool/vendor's fulfillment of stated administrative requirements. These administrative requirements were considered critical and were evaluated first—and in fact a majority of the tools were eliminated at this step.

TABLE 1 Fulfillment of Administrative Requirements

Survey Tool	Survey Monkey	Qualtrics	Key Survey	Checkbox	Opinion	Survey Share	SPSS Data Collection	Snap Survey
Site-wide License	✗	√	√	?	?	✗	✗	✗
Hosted Solution	√	√	√	√	√	√	√	✗
Automated Provisioning	✗	√	?	✗	✗	?	✗	✗
Web-Based Access	√	√	√	√	√	√	√	✗
Accessible Usage Metrics	✗	√	?	?	?	?	?	✗

It is important to note that Qualtrics was one of the first tools evaluated. Although it ultimately proved to be the only tool that could fulfill all administrative requirements (as is evident in Table 1), it also clearly influenced subsequent evaluations. Since a viable option was identified early, evaluators knew that they would not have to compromise on the presence of any administrative requirements. Therefore, they were able to completely eliminate tools that could not fulfill one or more administrative requirements without further evaluation of functional requirements.

The following tools/vendors were eliminated as options for the following reasons:

- *Survey Monkey*: It did not offer individual user accounts under a university-wide license. It did not offer automated account provisioning. It only offered licensing on a user-by-user basis, at a rate that would prove infeasible on a university-wide scale at NYU.
- *Snap Surveys*: Access is not Web-based and requires the user to download software. The software requires a Windows environment.
- *Checkbox*: It did not offer automated account provisioning.
- *Key Survey:* It only offered licensing that would prove infeasible on a university-wide scale at NYU. Automated account provisioning was untested by any of their other clients.
- *Survey Share*: It only offered licensing on a user-by-user basis at a rate that would prove infeasible on a university-wide scale at NYU.
- *SPSS Data Collections*: It did not offer automated account creation or management. It only offered pricing by number of survey respondents, which would prove infeasible on a university-wide scale at NYU.
- *Opinio*: It did not offer automated account provisioning.

Qualtrics was the only tool to fulfill all defined administrative requirements, while also meeting or surpassing all functional requirements.

SUPPORT MODEL OF THE NYU SURVEY SERVICE

Just as with any other large-scale service, the implementation of Qualtrics required a well-structured support model. The DSS already had a successful service model in place, supporting numerous quantitative, qualitative, and geographic research-based software packages; however, the mechanisms for the creation and collection of survey data were deemed deficient in many respects and demanded considerable revision. As a part of the Survey Tool and Service Evaluation Project, the DSS defined a scalable survey support model, the NYU Survey Service, with primary goals of providing sufficient technical support and training resources, as well as guidance on administrative procedures and research policies, to the faculty, staff, and students of NYU.

In order to "accommodate a variety of learning styles, including classroom instruction, small group coaching, individual appointments, and drop-in assistance" (Hurt 1997, 76), the NYU Survey Service offers survey support in both individual and group settings through one-on-one consultation sessions and classroom tutorials. Consultation sessions are available in person, on an appointment or walk-in basis, or remotely, via e-mail or telephone, anytime during the DSS's hours of operation. Group tutorials, led by DSS staff, and Webinars, provided by Qualtrics technical support, are routinely scheduled near the beginning of each academic semester, with additional sessions available upon demand. The DSS also recognizes the increasing importance of collaboration between faculty members and Library/ITS staff (Association of College and Research Libraries Research Planning and Review Committee 2010, 288) by working alongside professors to offer specialized in-class tutorials. In addition to providing individual and group training for Qualtrics, the NYU Survey Service extends its services to accommodate paper-based surveys by supporting the optical mark recognition software Remark OMR.

In creating the NYU Survey Service, DSS staff created and linked to a variety of reference resources for NYU patrons who have questions about survey creation or data collection. Documentation is available for each regularly scheduled tutorial provided by the DSS, and the NYU Survey Service research guide (http://nyu.libguides.com/survey), created with LibGuides, provides information for patrons seeking assistance with the use of survey software. The NYU Survey Service research guide also points to Qualtrics University (http://www.qualtrics.com/university/), a digital library of training resources hosted by Qualtrics. In addition to training resources, the NYU Survey Service guide contains valuable information on the policies and guidelines of the service, created and compiled by the NYU Survey Service team. This includes the NYU Survey Service Terms of Use, which lists the full set of requirements for using the service and highlights the need to consult the University Committee on Activities Involving Human Subjects (UCAIHS), NYU's institutional review board, for all research involving human subjects, as well as the requirement to follow the Office of Institutional Research and Program Evaluation's Survey Policy when surveying the NYU population.

Implementing the NYU Survey Service was a fairly seamless process; the DSS facilities (a computer lab loaded with specialty software) remained unaltered and the DSS support staff already believed that "ongoing staff training is a crucial component" (Cowgill, Beam, and Wess 2001) to a successful support model. "[Expecting] a high volume of questions on a wide range of topics varying in complexity from simple to the most advanced" (Graham 2003, 463), the DSS established a tiered support system where requests are assigned to the staff members who are best qualified to answer them; patrons are redirected to Qualtrics support when requests are beyond the capabilities of internal staff.

OUTREACH AND NEW RELATIONSHIPS

It was clear from the beginning of the project that to select and roll out a Web survey tool and service, the Data Service Studio would have to do a good deal of outreach—both in order to select the best tool to fit the needs of most users and to publicize the service once it was in place. This outreach was accomplished mainly via listservs, contacting known survey users, word of mouth through researchers and instructors who use the DSS, and preexisting ITS advisory groups. However, our efforts led us somewhat serendipitously to many survey users across campus. Through these contacts, we found a great deal of enthusiasm for a university-wide Web survey tool, and found that our full roll-out date could not come soon enough. Even though we have not had to work very hard to convince faculty of the tool's utility or importance, these outreach efforts gave us a welcome opportunity to promote other DSS services and generally get our name out to a wider audience on campus.

In addition to faculty, researchers, and instructors, we also forged a new relationship with the Office of Institutional Research and Program Evaluation (OIR), an administrative unit reporting to the Provost that conducts research to inform policy and planning at NYU. The OIR conducts a great deal of survey research, and it has been an enthusiastic early user of the NYU Survey Service; they also maintain a survey policy that applies to anyone wishing to survey NYU affiliates outside his or her own office or school. We first reached out to this group during our evaluation of Web survey tools, intending only to find out what tool or software they were currently using, but the relationship has proved mutually beneficial as we rolled out the service as well. By meeting the OIR staff members in Qualtrics training sessions and including them in our Qualtrics pilot period, we learned about their policy and have now included a pointer and link to it in the documentation for our service. The OIR readily agreed to this plan because they admitted that their survey policy is not yet widely known, and the link on our page will surely help them publicize it.

Another important collaboration that arose from the Web survey tool evaluation, selection, and rollout was that between the Data Service Studio and the University Committee on Activities Involving Human Subjects, which serves as NYU's institutional review board (IRB). Literature on collaborations between IRBs and libraries is scarce, but the few studies that exist, as well as others examining general tension between researchers and IRBs, tend to recommend fostering open communication between IRB members and researchers (Fitch 2005; Guss 2009; Labaree 2010). Libraries and librarians are well-positioned to carry out this liaison role, and this is especially true of a unit like the Data Service Studio; although ethics review is not explicitly mentioned in the DCC's Lifecycle Model, it is nonetheless a necessary and critical part of research involving human subjects. Our Web survey tool allows us to become more involved in this step of research, and even in promoting awareness and learning about the purpose and procedures of IRBs. After reaching out to the UCAIHS, we were able to meet with its chair and a senior administrator to explain our project and discuss how they might be affected. They were glad to have been notified and discussed creating boilerplate language about Qualtrics to provide to researchers for use in their IRB applications. A link to the UCAIHS's page and procedures is on our help documentation, along with a reminder that researchers should determine whether they need review prior to beginning their survey. The Web survey tool gave us a good opportunity to make contact with and get to know some members of this important university unit, which will continue to be beneficial beyond this single project.

As previously mentioned, the addition of a robust, widely available Web survey tool enables the Data Service Studio to support the data collection piece of the data life cycle at a higher level. In addition to filling in this one piece of the puzzle, providing a survey tool for educators and researchers helps us promote our other services and creates an in-road for us to be more intimately involved in other parts of the data life cycle as well. Establishing the DSS as the go-to place for survey research also advances our goals of developing and providing support to researchers planning for preservation of their research data for future use and reuse. Aside from interacting directly with users of the survey tool, our support documentation—which is currently in the format of a LibGuide library research guide—can contain information on archiving data and how the Libraries and DSS can help one do so. A Web survey tool is not only a valuable addition to our suite of services, but also a vehicle that has great potential to advance our other goals and projects related to collection and preservation of original research data created at NYU.

A final somewhat intangible yet very valuable benefit to providing a Web survey tool available to all faculty, students, and staff at the university is the increased visibility it is sure to bring to the Data Service Studio and, consequently, the Division of Libraries and ITS. In addition to attracting academic researchers and instructors of survey research methods to our services as a whole, the implementation of this survey tool has already attracted much attention from various university administrative units—many of which are heavy users of surveys themselves—and will surely continue to do so. It is likely that many of the administrators who use the NYU Survey Service will never have any other contact with us, but will now have heard of the DSS as a result of using this tool and service. Providing university-wide access to Qualtrics increases the Data Service Studio's visibility among administrators, educators, and researchers, and, therefore, our status as a valuable university entity—an increasingly vital position to strive for in an era of budget cuts and parsing of services.

Aside from the reasons we've outlined, the process of acquiring a Web survey tool and creating support services around it has produced a number of additional unanticipated benefits to the Data Service Studio in the form of outreach opportunities, new relationships, and promotion of the DSS as a whole across the university. Although these bonuses were not primary reasons for undertaking the project from the start, they may very well turn out to be significant reasons to continue the service into the future.

MOVING FORWARD WITH THE NYU SURVEY SERVICE

Now that the online component of the service is in place, the DSS has seen a growing number of accounts and requests for consultations or instruction, which we suspect will only grow as more users become aware of its existence. Undergraduates make up a portion of users in all these instances. It will be important to continue outreach efforts to all segments of the NYU population to ensure that the NYU Survey Service is being fully utilized. The introduction of the service allows us to support researchers at all levels in rigorous online survey research. At a time when the popular imagination is focused on the perceived or actual lack of resources for important societal needs, the discussion is likely to turn to the value of higher education (Dreifus and Hacker 2010; Houston 2008).

As a result, the library will need to maintain and assert its role as a center of information control and retrieval in order to counter the case for underinvestment. We are fortunate to have been in a position to make a case about the value of the survey service at a number of levels. Since survey research of one kind or another is ubiquitous at institutions of higher education, performing the type of cooperative, wide-ranging review that has been described here could be a mechanism toward cost-savings at other institutions, especially if multiple units are pursuing individual solutions as was the case at NYU. And, of course, there is the teaching and research mandate. Having a robust tool at the disposal of our affiliates allows teaching faculty to more easily supervise rigorous and responsible research by undergraduates and to give them greater flexibility to introduce the practice of such methodologies.

REFERENCES

Aldrich, D. M., and G. Stefanelli. 2006. Library services for a digital future. *Educause Quarterly* 29:70–73.

Association of College and Research Libraries Research Planning and Review Committee. 2010. 2010 top ten trends in academic libraries: A review of the current literature. *College & Research Libraries News* 71:286–92.

Atkinson, M. P., R. F. Czaja, and Z. B. Brewster. 2006. Integrating sociological research into large introductory courses: Learning content and increasing quantitative literacy. *Teaching Sociology* 34:54–64.

Card, J. J., L. Shapiro, A. Amarillas, E. McKean, and T. Kuhn. 2003. Broadening public access to data through the development of tools for data novices. *Social Science Computer Review* 21:352–59.

Cowgill, A., J. Beam, and L. Wess. 2001. Implementing an information commons in a university library. *The Journal of Academic Librarianship* 27:432–39.

Cozzens, M. B. 2003. Educational policy and decision making. In *Quantitative literacy: Why numeracy matters for schools and colleges*, ed. B. L. Madison and L. A. Steen, 197–98. Princeton, NJ: National Council on Education and the Disciplines.

Digital Curation Centre. 2010. Digital curation lifecycle model. http://www.dcc.ac.uk/resources/curation-lifecycle-model.

Doyle, J., and A. Mezzell. 2007. The undergraduate methods experience: Short-changing the future of political science. Paper presented at the American Political Science Association Teaching and Learning Conference, Charlotte, NC. http://www.apsanet.org/tlc2007/TLC07DoyleMezzell.pdf

Dreifus, C., and A. Hacker. 2010. *Higher education?: How colleges are wasting our money and failing our kids—and what we can do about it.* New York: Times Books.

Farrell, D., and J. C. Petersen. 2010. The growth of internet research methods and the reluctant sociologist. *Sociological Inquiry* 80:114–25.

Fitch, K. L. 2005. Difficult interactions between IRBs and investigators: Applications and solutions. *Journal of Applied Communication Research* 33:269–76.

Fricker, R. D., and M. Schonlau. 2002. Advantages and disadvantages of internet research surveys: Evidence from the literature. *Field Methods* 14:347–67

Graham, K. 2003. When the library becomes the largest computer lab on campus: Supporting productivity software in an academic environment. *College & Research Libraries News* 64:462–64, 468.

Green, A. G., and M. P. Gutmann. 2007. Building partnerships among social science researchers, institution-based repositories and domain specific data archives. *OCLC Systems & Services* 23:35–53.

Guss, S. 2009. Assessing the effects of institutional review boards on social science data archiving in digital repositories. Master's thesis, Univ. of North Carolina at Chapel Hill.

Higgins, J. J. 1999. Nonmathematical statistics: A new direction for the undergraduate discipline. *The American Statistician* 53:1–6.

Houston, D. 2008. Rethinking quality and improvement in higher education. *Quality Assurance in Education: An International Perspective.* 16:61–79

Hunter, A., S. L. Laursen, and E. Seymour. 2006. Becoming a scientist: The role of undergraduate research in students' cognitive, personal and professional development. *Science Education* 91:36–74.

Hurt, C. S. 1997. Building libraries in the virtual age. *College & Research Libraries News* 2:75–76.

Jordan, J., and B. Haines. 2006. The role of statistics educators in the quantitative literacy movement. *Journal of Statistics Education* 14, no. 2. www.amstat.org/publications/jse/v14n2/jordan.html.

Labaree, R. V. 2010. Working successfully with your institutional review board: Practical advice for academic librarians. *College & Research Libraries News* 71:190–93.

MacDougall, M. 2008. Ten tips for promoting autonomous learning and effective engagement in the teaching of statistics to undergraduate medical students involved in short-term research projects. *Journal of Applied Quantitative Methods* 3:223–40.

Madison, B. L. 2004. Two mathematics: Ever the twain shall meet? *Peer Review* 6:9–12.

Madison, B. L., and L. A. Steen. 2008. Evolution of numeracy and the National Numeracy Network. *Numeracy* 1:1–18.

McClure R., and S. Sircar. 2008. Quantitative literacy for undergraduate business students in the 21st century. *Journal of Education for Business* 80:369–74.

McGarry, D., and S. Guss. 2010. The NYU data service studio: A center for collaborative data services in the library. Poster presented at the International Association for Social Science Information Services & Technology (IASSIST) Conference, Ithaca, NY. http://ciser.cornell.edu/IASSIST/poster/ps2.shtm.

NYU Data Services Working Group. 2007. *Report of the data services working group: A data services model and implementation plans.* New York University.

Schield, M. 2004. Information literacy, statistical literacy, and data literacy. *IASSIST Quarterly* 28:6–11.

Shostak, S., J. Girouard, D. Cunningham, and W. Cadge. 2010. Teaching graduate and undergraduate research methods: A multipronged departmental initiative. *Teaching Sociology* 38:93–105.

Steen, L. A. 2004. *Achieving quantitative literacy: An urgent challenge for higher education.* Washington, DC: Mathematical Association of America.

Vandiver, D. M., and J. A. Walsh. 2010. Assessing autonomous learning in research methods courses: Implementing the student-driven research project. *Active Learning in Higher Education* 11:31.

Engaging the Campus Community Through New Roles and New Relationships: The McMaster University Library Postdoctoral Fellowship Program

JEFF TRZECIAK, JOHN MACLACHLAN, and NOAH SHENKER
McMaster University, Hamilton, Ontario, Canada

Recent reports identify a problem concerning university libraries—that of trending toward the disintermediation from the research process. Many experts have called for libraries to begin leading scholarship and to keep themselves relevant to faculty and students in light of recent work illustrating that within the hierarchy of answering questions regarding information evaluation and searching, librarians fall below Internet search engines, instructors, and even friends. In order to be successful and stay relevant, libraries must be reestablished as leaders within the university community. McMaster University in Hamilton, Ontario, Canada has taken the approach of "library as lab" by matching the needs of the library with the interests of an emerging scholar. This has led to the creation of three library-funded postdoctoral fellowships in a program sponsored by the Council on Library and Information Resources. The new positions have been successful in facilitating a greater number of university partnerships in both teaching and research through such initiatives as the creation of the Virtual Museum of the Holocaust and the Resistance and the opening of the Lyons New Media Center. The ongoing success of the postdoctoral initiative is insured with the creation of the McMaster Centre for Digital Scholarship.

INTRODUCTION

In April 2010, the Ithaka group released the results of their fourth annual survey of the attitudes and behaviors of faculty related to key issues for academic libraries (Head and Eisenberg 2010). The report, which can be found at http://www.ithaka.org/ithaka-s-r/research/faculty-surveys-2000-2009/faculty-survey-2009, indicates an ongoing trend toward the disintermediation of libraries from the research process. It identifies a "declining visibility and importance of traditional roles for the library and the librarian [which] may lead to faculty primarily perceiving the library as a budget line, rather than as an active intellectual partner" (13), and it calls on library leaders to "help *lead* scholars, in order to best support and facilitate scholarship as well as to ensure their own continuing relevance" (2).

At McMaster, we have participated in LibQUAL twice (2007 and 2010), a triennial survey of our students, faculty, and staff. Administered by the Association of Research Libraries, the LibQUAL survey captures data on user experiences and expectations of library services (see http://libqual.org/home for more information on LibQUAL). As in the Ithaka report, McMaster faculty responses in LibQUAL in 2007 demonstrated a preference for nonlibrary gateways for research. The results of this unpublished report were clear: on a daily basis, users start their search for information somewhere other than the library (See Figure 1 and Table 1).

The 2010 LibQUAL results indicated that faculty member use patterns of nonlibrary gateways have remained constant while graduate and undergraduate use of nonlibrary gateways has increased (See Table 2).

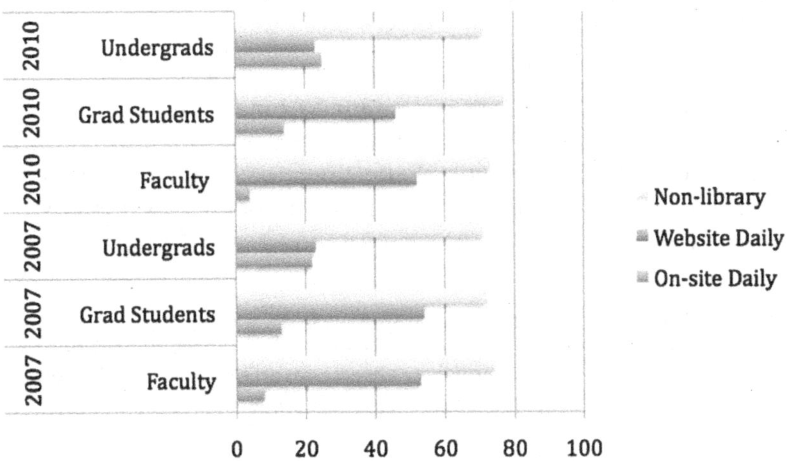

FIGURE 1 How McMaster University students, both graduate and undergraduate, and faculty access information according to the 2007 and 2010 LibQUAL surveys.

TABLE 1 Results from the 2007 LibQUAL Survey at McMaster University

	Used materials on-site daily	Used library Website daily	Used nonlibrary gateways
Faculty	8%	53%	74%
Graduate Students	13%	54%	72%
Undergraduates	22%	23%	71%

The McMaster University LibQUAL results correspond with those highlighted in the Ithaka report (Head and Eisenberg 2010), which states,

> faculty most often turn to network-level services, including both general purpose search engines and services targeted specifically to academia. These services have steadily grown in importance to a growing share of faculty members, and there is every reason to expect this pattern to continue. Although they may rely on resources licensed by the library, their pathway for discovery of these materials no longer goes through the library, except in a very technical sense; their access is only facilitated by the library "behind the scenes." (5)

It appears that faculty, who long ago began to move away from on-site use of the physical space of the library, may have also started to leave the virtual walls of the library as well. The McMaster University library is in danger of becoming a purchasing agent with minimal ties of any significance to the faculty.

Head and Eisenberg indicate a similar shift in the patterns of use among undergraduates, who they found "relied on librarians infrequently, if ever, whether they were conducting research for course work or for personal use" (2010, 8). Some of the specific findings include

- Students are much more likely to turn to a friend or family member for advice in evaluating information (61 percent) before an instructor (49 percent) or finally a librarian (11 percent).
- Librarians are used 30 percent of the time for searches of course-based material, far below friends (49 percent), Wikipedia (73 percent), Scholar Research databases (88 percent), and Internet search engines (92 percent).

TABLE 2 Results from the 2010 LibQUAL Survey at McMaster University

	Used materials on-site daily	Used library Website daily	Used nonlibrary gateways
Faculty	4%	52%	73%
Graduate Students	14%	46%	77%
Undergraduates	25%	21%	77%

- "Few students in the sample asked librarians (11 percent) or writing center staff (7 percent) for help when judging the information quality of sources for course work, and even fewer turned to librarians for help evaluating information for personal use (5%)." (13)

Traditionally university libraries have held a place as the "heart" of the academic communities we serve. We often referred to ourselves as the "lab," particularly for humanists. In the absence of any competition, we had a captive audience. Today we are facing stiff competition from Google and other information providers. Given the fiscal challenges plaguing our institutions, administrators are beginning to question the costs typically associated with managing a large research library. Circulation and reference services are in decline, and faculty are beginning to accept the consolidation and even closing of libraries.

In light of these shifts in user patterns and the other critical challenges facing academic libraries today, how do our libraries remain relevant in the eyes of our faculty and our students? What will libraries become when most of our materials can be downloaded to a smart phone or tablet? What will librarians become when communities of users are able to respond to individual inquiries? Libraries must clearly articulate our role and, in doing so, demonstrate real value.

We now have a unique opportunity to position ourselves as a pan-institutional lab. We are also in a period where our institutions remain supportive of the libraries but are beginning to question the value of our traditional activities in difficult economic times. The opportunity to reinvent ourselves will quickly disappear if we do not act. Windows of opportunity do not stay open long.

In order to be successful, libraries must reestablish ourselves as leaders working to address key challenges faced by our students and our faculty. Fortunately, our challenges—rapid technological development, a deluge of data and information, changing expectations and fiscal constraints, among others—are not unique. Libraries have much to offer in addressing these complex problems and should position ourselves as "leading the way" on our campuses. We are the perfect environment for studying how students learn and how faculty teach and conduct research in a rapidly evolving environment.

At McMaster we are taking the approach of "library as lab" by matching our needs with the interests of an emerging scholar and academic department. We have created three library-funded postdoctoral fellowships (PDF) modeled after the postdoctoral fellowship program sponsored by the Council on Library and Information Resources (CLIR). A fourth departmentally funded postdoc in classics will be cosponsored by the library to encourage collaboration with the library liaison for that department. The CLIR program "offers scholars the chance to develop new research models, collaborate with information specialists, and explore new career opportunities" (CLIR 2011). We hope that we can simultaneously support the development of emerging scholars while also addressing complex issues related to the discovery, creation, dissemination, and preservation of research.

The two-year program places the PDF with a senior faculty member in an academic department. Daily supervision of the PDF will take place within the library. Working in collaboration with the libraries, the PDF will continue her/his research while simultaneously contributing to an important initiative within the library. The benefit to the libraries, as articulated by CLIR, is that we gain access to the "expertise of accomplished scholars who can invigorate approaches to collection use and teaching, contribute field-specific knowledge, and provide insight into the future of scholarship" (CLIR 2011).

NEW RESEARCH COLLABORATIONS: THE CLIR POSTDOCTORAL RESEARCH FELLOWSHIP PROGRAM

McMaster University has embraced the changing roles of academic libraries, no longer envisioning those sites strictly as concrete, often insular repositories of traditional sources (such as microfilm, books, and journals) but also as virtual (as well as physical) spaces for developing works of digital scholarship in collaboration with both faculty and members of local, national, and international communities. To further its aims in that regard, the library has solidified a strong working relationship with the Council on Library and Information Resources (or CLIR), an independent, nonprofit organization that is committed to helping universities, archives, and cultural institutions create new policies and platforms for adapting to the evolving demands for information resources. One of the central strategies for addressing that challenge has been to facilitate the creation of Postdoctoral Fellowships in Academic Libraries across North America (CLIR PDFs). The first call for applications was posted in 2003 and resulted in fellowship postings at institutions including Princeton University, the University of Southern California, Yale University, Johns Hopkins University, and Bryn Mawr College. Recent placements have also included Lehigh University, Occidental College, the University of Nebraska-Lincoln, and three fellows currently in positions at McMaster University (Brunner 2009).

In keeping with the innovative strategic vision of McMaster University Library, and as reflective of new and emerging directions in digital librarianship, the CLIR PDFs have been placed at the university and other sites with the explicit aim to collaborate with faculty, librarians, and staff in activating change in the creation and transmission of academic research and innovative pedagogy that work in conversation with that scholarship.

Rather than looking at this challenge in terms of a singular discipline or academic institution, CLIR and its PDFs come from a wide spectrum of fields (physical anthropology, history, film and media studies, earth science, classics, and bibliographic studies, to name only a few) and conduct meetings with one another through both virtual conferencing and on-site meetings. Through this diversity of expertise and frequency of exchange, the fellows can better collaborate on developing networked approaches to advancing their respective projects under the larger umbrella of the CLIR goal of transforming the creation of, and access to, library and information resources. Synchronous virtual meeting sessions are conducted with both current and past CLIR PDF cohorts on a monthly basis to discuss issues ranging from IP/copyright to the challenges of providing incentives for digital scholarship and integrating its creation into traditional protocols for granting tenure and promotion.

The CLIR fellows are envisioned as "agents of change" intended to mobilize their doctoral expertise in facilitating a movement within libraries toward more innovative modes of scholarship and research access; the conceptualization of "change" is dialogic in terms of how it is forged in collaboration and conversation between CLIR fellows and the library faculty and staff (Brunner 2009). While the CLIR PDFs bring with them their own sets of experiences and conceptualizations of digital scholarship and its place in the library, the success of their work is contingent upon developing partnerships with innovative library staff members and university faculty who have the experiences of navigating their respective institutional landscapes and serving their diverse community of users. At the same time, it is precisely because the majority of CLIR Postdoctoral Fellows do not come from academic backgrounds in library and information studies that they are able to approach their projects with different, often innovative perspectives on how to transform digital scholarship and resource access. As the fellows immerse themselves in the challenges of developing new digital initiatives, they are, by necessity, compelled to develop experience in exploring matters of preservation, cataloging, indexing, user interface, and other fundamental tasks that they learn in partnership with their library staff colleagues. In short, the library and its staff benefit from the area expertise and outside perspectives of the PDF while at the same time helping fellows to cultivate their working knowledge of the inside culture and operations of the library in particular and the university at large. In addition, the interdisciplinary and flexible nature of the PDF's position—the fact that they are housed not only within libraries and archives but also often simultaneously appointed to academic departments with associated teaching and service opportunities—provides for a more integrated approach to developing digital projects. Rather than being limited to the creation of digital archives, they are active agents in forging and reimagining the larger strategic vision as well as the day-to-day archival and pedagogical responsibilities of the library.

Such has been the case with Dr. Noah Shenker, the first CLIR postdoctoral fellow appointed by McMaster University in the fall of 2009. Shenker was given the opportunity to coordinate the Virtual Museum of the Holocaust and the Resistance housed within the Archives and Research Collections of Mills Memorial Library. When completed, this dynamic online archive will feature collections recently acquired by the library, most notably an extraordinary collection of primary materials on the Holocaust assembled by Michel Brisebois of Montreal. The Virtual Museum will employ digital platforms to create an interactive archival infrastructure for preserving and accessing memoirs, official documents, postcards, ephemera, audiovisual testimony, and other original materials interlinked through thematic text, case studies, time-lines, maps, and bibliographies of events leading up to and immediately following the tragic events of the Holocaust (http://digitalcollections.mcmaster.ca/world-war-1939-1945-german-concentration-camps-and-prisons-collection).

Through its membership in The Task Force for International Cooperation on Holocaust Education, Remembrance, and Research, the Government of Canada has made Holocaust education a priority, and there is a growing need at many educational levels to present and understand this material through digital platforms (TFI 2011). With that in mind, Shenker has worked both within the library and across the university and local community to develop partnerships in preserving these invaluable resources. Most recently, the Virtual Museum has entered into discussion with both the Holocaust Education Centre of Toronto and the USC Shoah Foundation (a vast digital archive of audiovisual Holocaust testimonies) on codeveloping educational curriculum, scholarly programming, as well as public exhibitions (in the case of the former) and archival acquisition (in the case of the latter).

Though the Holocaust is the central event at the heart of the Virtual Museum, the moral and historical imperatives of that event are being preserved at McMaster with the aim of calling attention to past and ongoing genocides and human rights crises in places such as Armenia, Serbia, Cambodia, Rwanda, and Darfur, thereby impacting the experiences of immigrant and refugee groups who have arrived in Ontario and other parts of Canada and the United States. In that sense, the CLIR fellowship at McMaster provides an oppportunity for PDFs to engage not only within the physical space of the library, but also with the world outside the university.

NEW TEACHING COLLABORATIONS

From a pedagogical perspective, CLIR PDFs have been able to merge the information resources of the library and the scholarly mission of the university at large. Within McMaster University, PDFs such as Dr. Shenker and Dr. John Maclachlan serve as pedagogical facilitators, helping to identify and work with faculty who would not only be interested in collaborating on the creation of new digital scholarship projects, but who would also be interested in integrating preexisting digital tools at the university into their teaching practice. This facilitation lends itself to allow all McMaster CLIR PDFs to have numerous ties to teaching through the primary instruction of individual courses, course creation, working with individual course instructors to develop new assignments, working with faculties to facilitate skill development as a larger scale multicourse initiative, and involvement with university-wide multidisciplinary pedagogical projects. Successful extension of the library into the realms of teaching and learning will improve recognition of the library as a leader in addressing current university-wide challenges among undergraduate students, graduate students, and faculty.

In the winter term of 2010, Dr. Shenker, who has a faculty appointment both within the library and the Department of Religious Studies, identified the need to offer a course that addressed the representation and documentation of the Holocaust through various audiovisual media including film, television, new media, and archives, including the Virtual Museum of the Holocaust and the Resistance. The course, entitled Representations of the Holocaust, provided students with an opportunity to engage with the conceptual, ethical, and methodological questions that shape access to vital Holocaust sources and which, in turn, address the limits and possibilities of examining contemporary genocides through that historical and moral framework.

By working in collaboration with librarians, archivists, Web designers, and other crucial library staff, the Virtual Museum will serve as a nexus point for making accessible materials that might otherwise remain dormant within the library's collections. Ultimately, that is one of the primary goals of the CLIR Postdoctoral Fellowship in Academic Libraries and the current work of fellows at McMaster—to help identify library and information resources in need of cultivation and preservation, and to ensure that they are made relevant beyond the walls of the university through digital access as well as pedagogical and social practice.

The CLIR PDF appointment, The *Postdoctoral Research Fellow in New Media* position, held by Dr. Maclachlan, roughly coincided with the opening of the Lyons New Media Center (LNMC) in Mills Memorial Library in September 2010. This new and exciting space includes a help desk to assist with questions concerning new media including questions of software, video and audio editing workstations, a consultation space, a gaming theater, both a static and portable Green Screen, a 6' x 10' video wall, and a modern classroom (see http://library.mcmaster.ca/lyons for a detailed description). Within the LNMC, course instructors, staff, or individual students can book any of the separate components of the room for single use or on an ongoing basis for a course. This space and position bring with it new opportunities to promote the library as a space for skill development and the integration of digital media into teaching, learning, and research among students and faculty.

Within three months of the opening of the LNMC, numerous courses from a range of faculties including arts & sciences, health science, humanities, and social science had booked the classroom for ongoing use to allow for the further incorporation of new media beyond what would be possible in a traditional classroom on campus. Simply identifying which courses are booking rooms would not give a clear picture of how the space is being used. As a result of both formal and informal conversations with instructors, numerous courses across campus have adapted the traditional purely written essay style course capstone assignment to allow for all or a portion of an assignment to be created as a video, poster, or graphic novel in response to the creation of the newly acquired availability of appropriate software, hardware, and expertise provided by the library. Individual courses, such as *Inquiry into Climate Change*, a third-year course in the Faculty of Arts & Sciences, intend on using the video wall as a setting to disseminate final course projects to the university public within a conference style setting (examples of finished projects can be found at http://www.youtube.com/user/lyonsnewmedia). Many of the relationships with individual courses were facilitated through communications in which the CLIR PDF informed instructors of the unique opportunities available in the library and, more specifically, in the LNMC.

To expand the base of new media theory, literacy, and practical experience, a pilot program was developed in collaboration with the university's Faculty of Social Science. In order to reach as many students as possible, all first-year Social Science Inquiry courses (approximately two hundred and fifty students) offered during the fall 2010 term included 1.5 hours within the LNMC. Inquiry courses are created to be skill-driven rather than content-driven, with the focus of the courses on the development of skills that will assist students in performing well during their university years and beyond (see http://cll.mcmaster.ca/resources/inquiry.html). The mandate of skill development makes inquiry courses the ideal candidate to incorporate new media into skill development.

Each of the inquiry classes attended their LNMC session over a two-day period in October 2010. To keep the groups small and allow more time for contact with the instructor, each class was split into two sections with one section led by the CLIR PDF and the other by a library liaison, with the students switching at the midpoint of the session. The portion of the class working with the PDF was further split into two smaller groups and given a practical task of creating new media in either an audio format (a radio ad for the university) or a video commercial (a Web advertisement for McMaster). Instruction and limitations for the task were minimal, giving the students' creative freedom but ensuring them that assistance was always available for either theoretical or technical questions in an attempt to minimize any student frustration. The portion of the class working with the liaison librarian met in the LNMC classroom to increase their skill set in acquiring, referencing, and ethically using existing new media widely available on the Internet.

The majority of students were excited and engaged with the project, and it became quickly apparent that, as a group, the students both appreciated and excelled when given the opportunity to be creative in an academic setting. Students were asked to complete a survey to assess a baseline of perceptions toward the use of new media within university courses and the LNMC specifically. This one initiative resulted in increased visibility of the library for the two hundred and fifty students, ten instructors, and the faculty administrators who participated and showed how the library can be seen as a partner.

An extension to the inquiry course project was the creation of a larger scale version of the practical project using a single inquiry class, in conjunction with an individual instructor, and giving them more direction and more time to complete it (four hours instead of forty-five minutes). All first-year inquiry classes at McMaster have a unique theme that allows the instructors to organize the skill building inherent to the course. In this case, students were asked to create a five-minute news segment to report upon a current health issue, with the finished project being mandated to incorporate numerous aspects of new media representing both practical and theoretical ideas. All students were required to use the green screen and incorporate the footage as a portion of their report. Each of the four groups of six students used the green screen as the "anchor desk" for their news segments as they incorporated a traditional news desk setting as the background after filming. Students had to understand the ethical use of new media material and incorporate at least two images from creative commons (see http://creativecommons.ca), take and submit one still photograph, create a voice over as an introduction, and incorporate video that they created for the project all within a four-hour period. This was met with enthusiasm from the students as all groups managed to complete their videos within the allotted time frame. This project provided students the opportunity to gain and expand their new media skills, as they had to create primary material, efficiently search existing material, and use both hardware and software. This type of project would not have been possible at the scale provided without the expertise and equipment available from the LNMC.

An additional example of incorporation of the library into teaching and learning in an effort to lead scholarship is the libraries inclusion into large-scale university-scale collaborative projects such as the McMaster University Campus Wide Curriculum Initiative. This program will identify and develop common skills needed by all undergraduates to succeed both in and beyond their university careers. A series of self-directed multimedia modules is to be developed and accessed by students and followed at a pace comfortable to them. Modules are to be disseminated using the university's learning management system (Avenue to Learn or A2L) with completion noted on their transcripts. Topics are identified to create a path of success for future graduates in a globally knowledge-based economy, and they cover such topics as digital literacy (visual, media, geospatial), taking effective notes, time management, and presentation skills in multiple formats (text, video, data, etc). Partnership in this wide-scale ongoing initiative through the PDF program, with the LNMC as an intellectual partner to lead future scholars, will increase the visibility and student and faculty perception of the library moving forward.

CONCLUSION: THE BENEFITS AND CHALLENGES OF INTEGRAGING PDFS INTO ACADEMIC LIBRARIES

McMaster University Library

The assimilation of CLIR PDFs into the current structure of the McMaster University Library is a step in the right direction to address current questions of library perception among students and faculty and to facilitate integration as a partner of university research and teaching. Although this is a relatively new program, it has included the following successes:

- McMaster University Libraries CLIR PDFs show an effort to facilitate relationships among university faculty, staff, and students.
- Increasing the pedagogical contribution of the library will increase the visibility of the library to allow it to be seen as an intellectual partner.
- It has furthered the incorporation of active research into the library
- It has broadened the perception of the library as a valuable physical space through the active incorporation of teaching and research into the library.

All of these successes will play a role within the library of leading scholarship and forming partnerships with students and faculty, which are necessary for an academic library moving forward.

For the past four years the library has focused heavily on the development of "learning commons," spaces aimed at supporting teaching and learning at the undergraduate level. We have made significant investments in renovations, reorganizations of staff, and implementation of new technologies in support of learning. As a result, we have seen dramatic increases in the use of our facilities and services by undergraduates.

The same transformational technologies that have had a dramatic impact on teaching and learning are also altering research. Researchers are exploring new technologies, new strategies, and new relationships in the discovery, dissemination, and preservation of their research. New forms of scholarship are emerging such as e-books, open access journals, peer-reviewed blogs and wikis, dataset creation and publication, and other digital publications.

A recent donation for digitization and preservation provides the university with a unique opportunity to establish itself as a leader in the development of a center for digital scholarship and, in doing so, creates a "McMaster model" that others may emulate. The library, in collaboration with others across campus, took an important step in 2011 with the opening of the McMaster Centre for Digital Scholarship (MCDS), a campus-wide resource that fosters interdisciplinary research and development, supports collaborative experimentation and knowledge-sharing, and encourages innovative multimedia digital research. MCDS has become the administrative home for the postdoctoral research fellowship program, which will grow in time as the center grows. The program has already reinvigorated our library/faculty relationships even at this early stage. Our success in supporting research will depend upon our ability to sustain and grow this important emerging program.

Beyond McMaster University

Although this article has charted out some of the recent successes that McMaster University has had in integrating PDFs into the space of its library, there are broader implications and considerations to explore as other academic libraries move forward with similar initiatives.

One of the greatest assets that PDFs bring to an academic library is their doctoral expertise in a particular field. Rather than simply representing a credential in and of itself, the scholarly practice put into acquiring the PhD and maintaining an active scholarly profile serves as an invaluable asset in harnessing the academic potential of collections and resources housed within libraries. It is crucial that PDFs retain a dynamic teaching and research profile, including but not limited to the designing and teaching of relevant courses and the development of research projects that draw from the unique holdings and needs of their respective institutions. In addition to advancing the scholarly profile of individual PDFs, that continued scholarship and pedagogy help to facilitate a more collaborative dialogue between the library and other faculties across a university by positioning the library not as a site of traditional information dissemination, but rather as a partner in innovative teaching and research. To help further that aim of elevating the academic profile of the library, it is important for libraries to consider the possibility of more formally incorporating graduate students from diverse disciplines into their fold, especially if they possess research and teaching backgrounds relevant to certain collections and constituencies. Given the budgetary landscape of universities across Canada, such a measure would help spread the costs of funding graduate work, all the while giving the library much needed advanced area expertise with which to develop new research and teaching initiatives.

Another potential advantage that a PDF can bring to an academic library is the *absence* of training in library and information sciences. More precisely, as active members of the university and as scholars with an academic profile to maintain, PDFs are constantly engaged in the access, management, and integration of their own relevant sources and intellectual property, yet they are by and large untrained in the vital behind-the-scenes work of academic libraries. That "outsider" status is crucial if PDFs are to approach the changing demands of libraries with an eye toward meeting the demands of students, faculty, and members of the community without being tethered to traditional library hierarchies and roles. Although it is crucial for PDFs to learn from and work in collaboration with skilled librarians, staff, and other professionals within the library, the PDF designation, which is aptly defined as being both of and outside the traditional boundaries of a library, is key to facilitating change.

REFERENCES

Brunner, M. L. 2009. Ph.D. holders in the academic library: The CLIR Postdoctoral Fellowship Program. In *The expert library: Staffing, sustaining, and advancing the academic library in the 21st century* (pp. 158–179), ed. S. Walter, V. Coleman, and K. Williams, Chicago: Association of College and Research Libraries.

Council on Library and Information Resources (CLIR). 2011. Postdoctoral fellowship in academic libraries 2011. http://www.clir.org/fellowships/postdoc/postdoc.html.

Head, A. J., and M. B. Eisenberg. 2010. *TRUTH BE TOLD: How college students evaluate and use information in the digital age.* Project Information Literacy Progress Report, November 1.

TFI. 2011. Task Force for International Cooperation on Holocaust Education, Remembrance, and Research. http://www.holocausttaskforce.org/.

Cool Collaborations: Designing a Better Library Experience

ROBERT FOX
University of Louisville, Louisville, Kentucky, USA

CATHY CARPENTER and AMEET DOSHI
Georgia Institute of Technology Libraries, Atlanta, Georgia, USA

Academic libraries routinely partner with other campus units in such areas as information literacy or writing support. However, the Georgia Tech library collaborations described in this article step outside the norm in that librarians are involved throughout the process of designing the collaborative projects; the projects are integrated into the undergraduate curriculum and embrace the science, technology, and design campus focus; the library incurs little or no financial commitment; and projects are ongoing or have long-term effects. The projects continue to change campus perceptions of libraries and librarians, and they have made the library a sought after "cool" collaborator on campus.

Founded in 1885 as the Georgia School for Technology, the Georgia Institute of Technology is a science and technology university that produces engineers, architects, scientists, and industrial designers—a school where the design process is infused into the curriculum. Established as a strictly baccalaureate institution, Georgia Tech today has established an international reputation as a graduate research institution. Over 7,000 of its 21,000 students are graduate students and one-half of its income is derived from research funding. Despite this strong research emphasis, Georgia Tech places great importance on its undergraduate programs. Evidence of this importance includes an active undergraduate research program, a position of prominence for undergraduate studies in the institute's new strategic plan, and the Clough Undergraduate Learning Commons (Clough Commons, or CULC), scheduled to open fall 2011, which colocates undergraduate academic and technology support services with all science labs for first- and second-year students. The Clough Commons is being constructed so that it connects to the main Georgia Tech library.

Georgia Tech's main library facility consists of two separate buildings joined by a four-story bridge. A branch library is located in the College of Architecture. The library has pursued significant physical and programmatic improvements that have made it a very popular campus destination for undergraduate students, and the library's transformation earned it the 2007 Association of College and Research Libraries Excellence in Academic Libraries Award.

This transformation was aided through work with campus partners. Like most academic libraries, the Georgia Tech library has historically collaborated with other campus units to improve resources and services, and this has only become more important in the recent period of fiscal constraint shared by many libraries. The Georgia Tech library has sought out and continues to maintain traditional forms of collaboration such as partnering with faculty to provide information literacy courses or to support a writing center, sponsoring student events and faculty lectures, or serving as a venue for art exhibits and performances. However, in recent years, the library has sought out more nontraditional collaborations.

A search in the academic library literature reveals that, although numerous articles have been written about collaborative activities, much of this work is focused on interlibrary collaborations such as interlibrary loan, cooperative collection development, and related consortia projects (Maskell, Soutter, and Oldenberg 2010). Furthermore, the literature on academic library outreach indicates that significant work has already been performed in collaborating with writing centers and humanities-oriented campus partners (Mahaffy 2008). Pan, Valliant, and Reed (2009) discuss similar partnerships with academic advisors to promote information literacy initiatives. Love and Edwards (2009), at the University of Illinois, write about reaching out to a wider array of student service organizations such as multicultural student groups or career services. Their goal is to find opportunities to expand the library brand and spread information literacy principles in nontraditional environments outside of the library facility. The most relevant book on the topic of academic library collaborations, *Libraries Within Their Institutions: Creative Collaborations*, is a compilation of articles about collaborating with writing centers and working with teaching faculty to help embed information literacy principles and cooperative digitization projects (Miller and Pellen 2004). While such partnerships are valuable and important to most academic libraries, the projects we discuss in the following sections are low-cost, design-oriented, nontraditional, and often make permanent or semipermanent changes to the library space. Our review of the academic library literature reveals that such research has not been shared to date. This article seeks to fill a gap in the literature by presenting examples of innovative or "cool" collaborative activities that help to reinvent the library's image among undergraduate students and others on campus. Given the relative lack of professional literature on the subject, our focus is to showcase successful nontraditional collaborative activities by the Georgia Tech library. We address how the library developed these collaborations to help build and inform partnerships with campus units that would be located in the CULC, to take advantage of the embedded nature of the architecture library, and to challenge campus perceptions of the roles of libraries and librarians.

Expanding on traditional librarian outreach efforts or space programming that utilizes the library solely as a venue, the "cool" collaborations noted below share many of the following features:

- projects are integrated into the undergraduate curriculum;
- library staff are involved in project design;
- projects embrace the science, technology, and design campus focus;
- projects incur little or no library financial commitment; and
- projects are of an ongoing nature or make physical changes to the library rather than being ephemeral.

In the next sections we describe five highly successful "cool" collaborations that share these features and that have positioned the library for additional collaborative opportunities.

COOL COLLABORATION: ACCESSIBLE AQUARIUM PROJECT

In the spring and summer of 2010, the library collaborated with Georgia Tech's Center for Assistive Technology and Environmental Access (CATEA) to house a "virtual aquarium" project within the library space (see Figure 1). The goal of the "virtual aquarium" project is to make aquarium and other museum experiences more accessible, in this case, for the visually impaired.

Using a video camera that applies metadata to moving objects, the technology identifies and tracks different species of fish and then assigns a musical instrument to each species. So, for example, a clownfish could sound like a trumpet and a manta ray might be assigned the sound of a cello. The software also changes pitch and tempo based on the movement of the fish, thus creating a symphony of sounds based on the real-time movement of different species of fish in the tank. For someone who might be visually impaired, this technology offers a unique way to experience an aquarium. The technology can also be applied to other environments such as zoos and museums, and instead of musical sounds, the objects

FIGURE 1 Students interacting with the "Accessible Aquarium" in the library, 2nd floor, West Commons.

can be coded as narration or other forms of output. Although CATEA is a center dedicated to discovering innovative assistive technologies for those who might be handicapped in some way, these projects can inspire all to experience sensory environments in creative new ways.

Once per year, the Georgia Tech research community shares its output in a research showcase. In the fall of 2009, a member of the library's User Experience department attended the research showcase and demonstrated a particular interest in the CATEA virtual aquarium project described above. One of the primary investigators for this National Science Foundation (NSF)-funded project noted that NSF requires user feedback as part of the grant request, and they were struggling with finding a location on campus to solicit feedback from a wide cross-section of individuals. The researchers wanted to observe how users of all abilities and backgrounds (not just those with visual impairments) interact with the aquarium project. Given the Georgia Tech library's centrally located facility and the large numbers of students who use the space, we offered the library as a potential space for gathering user feedback about the aquarium project. It is notable that a spring 2010 LibQUAL+ survey indicated that 65 percent of all undergraduates utilize the library facility on a daily or weekly basis, and 88 percent of all undergraduates use the facility at least monthly. Thus, the library offers the potential to reach a huge cross-section of undergraduate students.

The researchers indicated that they would require a mobile LCD screen and a computer to run a simulation of the aquarium. Members of the library staff worked with the Office of Information Technology to assess technology needs for hosting the project and determined that it would be possible to temporarily repurpose existing mobile LCD screens in the library. This enabled CATEA staff to upload the necessary software to display the "eye-catching" virtual aquarium and, ultimately, capture the attention of library users to gain needed feedback about the project.

This collaboration illustrates how the library embraces the science and technology focus of the Institute, and portrays itself as being open to collaborative research on campus. The virtual aquarium requires minimal staff time and also leverages existing resources, thereby incurring no financial commitment from the library. Furthermore, this on-going project creates a new line of communication between the library and CATEA, which opens up possibilities for additional unique collaborations. For example, students affiliated with CATEA have discussed working with the library to assess and improve the library's touch-screen technologies and signage to make them more accessible for patrons with visual impairments. This collaboration leverages existing resources to minimize costs, while positioning the library as a place where users can interact with "cool" research. Furthermore, these types of collaborations transform library spaces from being simply another study location on campus into an extension of a laboratory space where active learning can and does occur.

COOL COLLABORATION: VIRTUAL POSTER SESSIONS FOR UNDERGRADUATE RESEARCH

The mobile LCD screens utilized for the aquarium project have been useful for a number of internal library projects as well as other library collaborations. For example, the library maintains a strong relationship with the Office of Undergraduate Studies, which is focused on assessing and improving the undergraduate experience at the institute. Many of the highest achieving undergraduates are identified by the Office of Undergraduate Studies for prestigious scholarships and fellowship opportunities such as the Marshall, the Fulbright, and the Rhodes. The library frequently features these high achieving undergraduates (who are also typically heavy library users) on large posters noting their achievements and how they use the library.

During the spring 2010 semester, the Office of Undergraduate Studies expressed an interest in finding a space and mechanism to highlight undergraduate students who work with faculty on current research projects. We met with the director of the office and brainstormed possibilities for engaging formats to present undergraduate research. One of the spaces that is often used for such presentations is the Library East Commons or LEC. The LEC space is a recently renovated area of the library that offers students flexible furniture (movable chairs and tables), adjustable lighting options and technologies that facilitate collaboration. Undergraduate students heavily use the space at all hours. We considered a variety of locations but determined that this LEC space, because of its popularity among undergraduates, would be the ideal location for an undergraduate research showcase. Next, we brainstormed options for showcasing undergraduate research. One possibility that we discussed involved a series of live poster sessions, whereby the space would be reserved at regular increments and students would discuss their research with passers-by (similar to the model used at many conferences). Although we agreed that the potential for personal contact between students conducting research and their peers would be a valuable outcome, the logistics of scheduling multiple "live" poster sessions could prove cumbersome with no guarantee that students in the LEC would demonstrate any interest in engaging with those presenting their work. An ad-hoc committee formed to facilitate this collaboration determined that a more preferable option to the live, in-person sessions would be "virtual" poster sessions (see Figure 2).

FIGURE 2 Virtual Poster Session for Undergraduate Research located in Library East Commons.

The LCD monitors could be preloaded with undergraduate students presenting their work and could be set up such that the presentations would run continuously in the LEC space. This arrangement was advantageous for a number of reasons. First, it would require less staff time and resources; second, the Office of Information Technology was able to procure additional LCD screens for this purpose at no cost to the library; and third, the poster sessions would run numerous times so that more students could have an opportunity to see their peers' research work.

This virtual poster session collaboration with the Office of Undergraduate Studies demonstrates how library staff are continuously involved with the project design and execution. This project also embraces the research focus of the institute while requiring minimal financial commitment from the library. Most significant, however, is the fact that this project connects with undergraduate students in an area that aligns closely with the institute's emphasis on undergraduate research and student engagement.

COOL COLLABORATION: "STRESSBUZZTERS"—STRESS RELIEF FOR FINAL EXAMS

The week preceding final exams at Georgia Tech is colloquially known as "Dead Week" among the students. Cramming for exams during Dead Week is a Georgia Tech tradition and students sometimes can and do buckle under the strain. This time is particularly challenging for new undergraduate students who have typically not been exposed to such an intense period of stress. Since fall 2009, the library has been collaborating with the Counseling Center, the Campus Recreation Center, and the Health Promotions Office on an event called "StressBuzzters" aimed to help relieve the strain facing students. The branding for the StressBuzzters program is a play on words involving the Georgia Tech mascot, Buzz. StressBuzzters takes place in a popular library commons group collaboration area one evening during Dead Week for two to three hours. Library staff, counselors, and staff from the health promotions office and recreation center convene to distribute health snacks, bottled water, stress balls, and provide free chair massages to students studying in the library (see Figure 3). Librarians are also on hand to help students with last-minute research questions, while counselors offer advice on stress management and techniques to help deal with test anxiety.

This collaboration has proven to be very popular and requires only a minimal financial commitment from the library (about $150 for fruit snacks, bottled water, and granola bars). In spite of the fact that the event has only happened twice, students are already aware of StressBuzzters and word spreads very quickly about the free chair massages and snacks. During a period of intense anxiety, the library is viewed as being compassionate to the needs of students, thereby challenging often common, though unfortunate,

FIGURE 3 Massage therapist volunteering in library during final exams as part of "StressBuzzters"

perceptions about the academic library. Finally, this is an ongoing collaboration, and discussions about how to most appropriately expand StressBuzzters to include more partners and serve more students are under way.

COOL COLLABORATION: "LOST IN THE STACKS"—THE LIBRARY ROCK N' ROLL RADIO SHOW

In January 2010, the User Engagement Librarian and the Library's East Commons Coordinator collaborated with Georgia Tech undergraduate students to launch the first "research library rock n' roll radio show" on WREK 91.1 FM Atlanta. WREK is Georgia Tech's student radio station and was founded in 1968. The station is operated entirely by students and is funded by the Student Government Association.

This unique collaboration began as an attempt to market library events and resources via brief one or two minute public service announcements on the student station. Eventually the idea morphed into a full-fledged radio program that explores different library-related themes each week. The radio show is called "Lost in the Stacks" and broadcasts live at noon every Friday. The show is a mix of interviews with students, faculty, and library staff with

FIGURE 4 Co-hosts Ameet Doshi (2nd from left) and Charlie Bennett (far right) interview a Georgia Tech student and faculty member on "Lost in the Stacks."

theme-related music (see Figure 4). As an example, a show with the theme of "The Library and Film" included interviews with the librarian responsible for developing the library's film collection, undergraduate students from the film club about how they use the library as a location for their films, and a faculty member about her use of the library's scholarly film resources. Each interview is divided up by a set of theme-related music. For the show about "Libraries and Film," each music set included songs about films or related to the process of filmmaking (for example, "Clark Gable" by The Postal Service and "Favorite Films" by Television Personalities). Producing each week's show involves between two and three hours of research and recording, as well as brainstorming about theme-related music.

The process of obtaining a regular slot on the weekly rotation involved communication within the library, as well as with the student leadership of the station. The hosts were first asked to submit a written proposal about the program to WREK and then record a "pilot" episode for evaluation by the WREK executive board. Fortunately, a number of students indicated an interest in the idea and offered their production skills to help record the first pilot episode and serve as board operators each week. Every program on WREK requires a student board operator controlling the technical aspects of the show and many students sit in on the show each week to offer their opinions and ideas about libraries. Because student schedules can be erratic, we needed to recruit three or four back-up student operators who would be willing and able to step in at the last minute if needed.

To help market the program a Website was created (http://lostinthestacks.org) to direct users to the show's Facebook page. As of November 2010, the site has more than 400 fans on Facebook, many of whom actively communicate their thoughts about "Lost in the Stacks" on the Facebook wall. Not surprisingly, a large portion of the Facebook fans (and, presumably, listeners) are Georgia Tech undergraduate students. The show is archived for one week on the WREK Webpage, and many of the interviews are archived in podcast format in SMARTech, the library's institutional repository. A future goal for the program is determining how to legally distribute the entire show, including the copyrighted music, via a "Lost in the Stacks" podcast. Because of the complex legal issues involved, such distribution will require additional research and resources before it becomes a reality. Nonetheless, the show has garnered attention within the library community, as well as among undergraduate students at Georgia Tech. Our listener evaluations suggest that the radio program has been a successful, low-cost, high-impact collaboration with student media that helps shape user perceptions of the Georgia Tech library and library staff in new and positive ways.

The show does involve some costs since the hosts purchase music for the program on their own; however, there is no cost to the library other than the commitment of staff time by the two cohosts. The collaboration leverages existing infrastructure and uses free marketing methods (such as Facebook and Twitter) to gain listeners. Most importantly, although "Lost in the Stacks" is, to our knowledge, the first such library radio program, our hope is that we inspire other academic libraries to engage their users in similar "cool" ways.

COOL COLLABORATION: DESIGNING AND CONSTRUCTING A DISPLAY WALL

The Georgia Tech College of Architecture library is the only branch library on campus. The architecture program, started over one hundred years ago, was one of the first such programs in the south. As the college's buildings have not been renovated in thirty years, classrooms are straining to accommodate the large increase in architecture students and their unique needs for studio and gallery space.

The architecture librarian was aware of the shortage of gallery space and thought it would be a good idea to use library space to exhibit student work. The librarian conceived of a project to have architecture students design and construct a structure to display exhibits in the library. It would be less expensive than purchasing a prefabricated display unit and would result in a unique structure that would make a great collaborative project between the library and the architecture students. The Associate Dean of the Library, a strong believer in library collaborations, approved the idea and provided $1,000 to fund materials.

The Dean of the College of Architecture (COA) also supported the idea. He thought it would be a good active learning project for the students and was pleased that the library could provide money for a course titled Exhibiting Construction, which provided an opportunity to develop the project. Twelve students enrolled in the course that was offered as an elective during fall semester 2009.

During the semester, the students met regularly with the architecture librarian. The process of designing a building, space, or a structure usually consists of several design phases. During the first meeting, the students questioned the librarian about what she wanted for the exhibit structure. Her goal was to have a display structure built behind an eighteen foot long metal freestanding bookshelf. It would need to be flexible enough to display various types of artistic media—three-dimensional student work such as models and sculpture, as well as one-dimensional drawings. It would need to have some shelves to hold heavy models yet be able to display an exhibition of photographs. She envisioned several types of exhibits: student and faculty displays, library curated exhibits such as scanned drawings from the library's archives, and special themed exhibits.

Several weeks later, the schematic design phase began where students focus on creating the overall scheme. During the "pin-up" session with the librarian, the students showed her their digital designs. The students had a range of wonderfully creative ideas. However, many of the proposals were not realistic given the limited materials budget and the short period of time that the students had to construct and install the structure before the end of the semester. The instructor did her job of keeping the students on task and narrowing down the options to something that was practical.

The library was built in the early 1980's with a contemporary, industrial look that was popular at the time, with features such as an open ceiling with exposed pipes and abundant natural light. One of the students knew someone who worked at a steel company. She told them about the class project and the company offered to donate the steel. Steel, although an unusual material for an exhibit structure, was the perfect material for the library space. It provided a simple and unobtrusive background to whatever would be on display.

The development phase began as the overall scheme was refined into the final design. The plan was to use six panels of grey steel and attach each panel to the back of the metal bookshelf with magnets. Twenty-six steel shelves were fabricated in various sizes. The students had never worked with steel as a design material and found it quite challenging. Finally, the construction phase began (see Figure 5) and the installation was completed by the end of the semester.

FIGURE 5 Construction of exhibit wall in the architecture library.

Upon completion of the exhibit wall, the librarian contacted several faculty to see who would like to use it to display student work. The first exhibit featured student models of New Orleans houses designed to be inexpensive and eco-friendly. The second exhibit featured sculptural/geometric white models from a course on architectural scripting and pattern formation (see Figure 6). The response to the exhibit wall by faculty, administration, and students has been overwhelmingly favorable. People have commented on

FIGURE 6 Completed exhibit wall in the architecture library.

the uniqueness of using steel as the material and the clever use of magnets to attach the removable shelves. The overall look of the steel wall fits perfectly with the contemporary style of the library.

Several positive consequences resulted from the exhibit wall project. The students earned course credit while actively participating in a practical learning and design experience. For the librarian, the students in the class served as an informal focus group to provide feedback about the library's collection, services, and policies. She also developed relationships with the students that changed their perception of her from being a librarian whom they did not know to now seeing her as a colleague. The administration and faculty appreciate the wall so much that it has been used as a backdrop for interviews and photos. The Dean of COA had a professional photographer take photos of him sitting in the library with the exhibit wall in the background, and a professor who wrote a bestselling book has used the library space twice during interviews filmed for PBS programs.

Another consequence of having a successful collaboration is that it can often lead to other worthwhile collaborations. The library's Sustainability Committee had wanted to obtain recycling bins to put on each floor in the library. Students today are environmentally aware and some of them had requested containers to recycle their papers while studying in the library. Georgia Tech has an Industrial Design program and a collaborative project was proposed to the professor of the senior design course. The library offered a minimal amount of funding for materials if the students could design and construct the recycling containers as part of a class assignment. Again, here is a win-win project where the library obtains something of use and the industrial design students get to design an object that serves a real purpose.

CONCLUSION

Each of the projects presented above represents a successful collaboration between the library and others on campus. Each project shared our noted themes of integration with the undergraduate curriculum, embracing the institute's science, technology, and design focus, library staff involvement in the project design, little or no library financial commitment, and an end result with lasting effect.

Along the way, we have learned some lessons in building successful collaborations involving faculty and undergraduate students. These include the following:

- Students are very busy and cannot be expected to commit to a library project just for fun. Many successful projects are tied to course credit or with themes to which the students personally identify.

- When proposing a project, ensure there is buy-in from administrators as well as faculty members to help move the project forward in a timely manner.
- Offer some incentive (library space, seed funds, increased visibility, etc.) that will reflect the library's commitment and will help kick off the project.
- Although some collaborations may require only an initial time investment, others will involve a continual commitment. Library staff working on such long-term collaborations should prepare to manage their time and resources accordingly.
- Because many of our collaborations are unique, assessing the impact and success of these projects can be challenging. For these projects, a mix of quantitative data as well as anecdotal and qualitative comments can help provide a clearer picture of their impact. For example, with the "Lost in the Stacks" radio program, we rely on both the demographic and statistical data supplied by Facebook (in the "Insights" data tab), as well as user comments on the Facebook wall and comments received directly from students.
- Marketing these collaborative projects to the wider campus community creates both a challenge and an opportunity. As with many library projects, penetrating through the "noise" of other campus events is difficult. However, it is possible to leverage the marketing talents of your campus partners to promote the project via a variety of different channels, thereby reaching a more diverse student demographic.

These are challenging times for academic libraries. Some librarians may view the future with trepidation but we see this time as one of opportunity. Developing collaborations increases the library's visibility and usage and can significantly strengthen the role of the library within the educational institution. One reason for the Georgia Tech library's success has been the library's culture of innovation and risk taking that has allowed us to seek nontraditional partners. The library also benefits from the perception of neutrality among students and faculty in an increasingly interdisciplinary campus environment. These successful partnerships have changed perceptions of what role the library can play for undergraduate success and have set us apart as the "cool" collaborator on campus.

REFERENCES

Love, E., and M. B. Edwards. 2009. Forging inroads between libraries and academic, multicultural and student services. *Reference Services Review* 37:20–29.

Mahaffy, M. 2008. Exploring common ground: US Writing Center/Library Collaboration. *New Library World* 109:173–81.

Maskell, C., J. Soutter, and K. Oldenburg. 2010. Collaborative print repositories: A case study of library directors' views. *Journal of Academic Librarianship* 36:242–49.

Miller, W., and R. Pellen. 2004. Libraries within their institutions: Creative collaborations. Binghamton, NY: Haworth Information Press.

Pan, D., M. Valliant, and B. Reed. 2009. Creative collaboration: Developing a partnership with an academic advisor to promote information literacy and student success. *College & Undergraduate Libraries* 16:138–52.

The Third Place: The Library as Collaborative and Community Space in a Time of Fiscal Restraint

SUSAN E. MONTGOMERY and JONATHAN MILLER
Olin Library, Rollins College, Winter Park, Florida, USA

In a period of fiscal constraint, when assumptions about the library as place are being challenged, administrators question the contribution of every expense to student success. Libraries have been successful in migrating resources and services to a digital environment accessible beyond the library. What is the role of the library as place when users do not need to visit the building to utilize library services and resources? We argue that the college library building's core role is as a space for collaborative learning and community interaction that cannot be jettisoned in the new normal.

The "new normal" is a period of fiscal constraint in which assumptions about the library as place are being challenged. The phrase, in its current sense of a long-term shift from one set of business conditions to another, has been around since the dot.com bust of 2001. The phrase was first used in this current iteration by Roger McNamee, a venture capitalist and something of a guru in the new media and information technology fields (Fast Company 2002). However, the phrase has been used to describe new long-term business conditions or changed circumstances since at least the recession of the early 1990's (Davis 1990; Gwyn 1992). The term generally has connotations of tougher times in which we are exhorted to concentrate on business fundamentals rather than quick profits and visionary schemes. In this sense, it is a useful way to think about librarianship in the second decade of the

21st century. Since the recession of 2007, most academic libraries have found themselves in a period of fiscal constraint as the institutions they serve and that fund them face budget cuts, calls to restrain tuition increases, declining revenues, and lower income from endowments.

There is, however, another sense in which librarianship and libraries find themselves in a new normal. Over the last four decades, academic libraries have been extraordinarily successful in migrating from analog, or print-based, services and collections toward digital, networked services and collections. We have now reached the point at which most, if not all, academic libraries in the United States are now hybrid operations of both analog and digital services and collections, and many libraries are beginning to contemplate a purely legacy role for their print collections.

In a hybrid information environment in which the digital dominates, and an economic environment in which institutions face the long-term prospect of tight budgets, administrators question the contribution of every expense to the bottom-line of student success. Essentially, the question is—what is the role of the library as a physical place when users do not need to visit a library building to use library services or resources? Administrators are not alone in asking this question. Ironically, in an age in which much of our lives has moved into a digital space, physical space remains the coin of the realm in higher education. Faculty members, if they have not already done so, are eager to recapture space in academic buildings previously devoted to departmental libraries. Main library facilities, often occupying prime real estate at the center of campus, have also become contested spaces with some faculty members questioning the continuing relevance of such enterprises (Ithaka 2009), and others conducting rear-guard actions against remote storage of print collections by demanding that all books remain on the central campus (Howard 2009).

Students are voting with their feet and conducting their library research from any wired or wireless networked location. The old librarian's lament at seeing a senior enter the library for the first time is no longer relevant. In many cases it is now possible for students to graduate having made full use of the library's digital resources and services from locations outside of the library. Unless librarians create conditions under which the library building is used for something other than information retrieval, students will continue to move elsewhere.

We argue that the core role of the library building in the next decade will not be as a storehouse of collections or as a central point of information service, although in our hybrid environment it will continue to play both those roles. The core role of the library as a place, the new normal for library buildings, is as a place of collaborative learning and community interaction. Further, we argue that this role cannot be jettisoned during a time of fiscal constraint. Librarians must not use the new normal as an excuse for retrenchment. This not only makes practical economic and educational sense, but is also historically grounded in the ancient role of libraries as places of community and collaboration, a history that, in the twentieth century, had been put aside as print collections ballooned during the information explosion of the second half of the twentieth century and the use of library space moved from people to print.

As users increasingly gained the ability to use library services and collections from outside the library building, and as libraries faced increased competition from online information service providers, academic librarians focused on marketing and advocacy as a way to entice users back into the library building. A review of an early bibliography of marketing in libraries and of records in EBSCO's Library, Information Science, and Technology Abstracts (LISTA) database shows an early concern among librarians to market innovative online mediated search systems in the 1970's (Norman 1989). As early as 1980 Edinger argued for marketing as a strategy for library survival (1980). And in 1982 Cronin argued that the "electronic information age" required librarians to market their services.

The most prominent example of this marketing trend is the Association of College and Research Libraries' (ACRL) marketing campaign @Your Library (ACRL 2010). That campaign markets the library and seeks to inform people about the continuing importance of librarians in education and research. In addition, it aims to increase the visibility of librarians and promote librarianship as a career. However, from the very branding of the campaign—@Your Library, which plays with a symbol that connotes both digital (e-mail) and place "at"—the physical library is an integral part of the campaign.

However, it is our contention that, in the face of a historic societal trend from print to digital, a trend that continues to transform our sense of community, place, geography, and space throughout our lives, we cannot persuade our users to return to a way that is inconvenient and no longer necessary. Marketing library services that remain relevant to users is important, but simply marketing the library as a worthy place on our campuses will not bring users back into the library building. Instead we must fulfill the continuing needs of our users for information organization, access, instruction, and assistance in new ways that take into account the new realities, and we must do the same with library space. In the traditional sense, we cannot *market* the importance of the library as place to our users; we must *be* an important place in their lives. As Brian Matthews, formerly the User Experience Librarian at Georgia Institute of Technology, and now Assistant University Librarian at UC Santa Barbara, put it in his ground-breaking book *Marketing Today's Academic Library*, "We must demonstrate our value through applied relevance, instead of fabricating implied needs. On a grand scale, we need to stop thinking in terms of the user being in the library and instead consider how the library fits into the life of the user" (2009, 2).

The important role for college and undergraduate library spaces, when less space is needed to house collections, the role that our users want us to play in their lives, is as flexible spaces for collaborative work and in which they can be part of a self-created community.

This argument is not entirely new. The changing role of "library as place" has been a growing concern throughout the first decade of the twenty-first century. A 2003 article by Bennett surveyed academic library directors who supervised building renovations during the 1990s. In it he characterized the library as a "service place" and as a "learning place." The library as a "service place" is the traditional view of the building where information is held, organized, and managed. The concept of the library as a "learning space" recognizes that the main activity and focus of the library is "facilitating social exchanges through which information is transformed into the knowledge of one person or group of persons" (4). The fundamental change Bennett addressed in his research is the way in which people's use of the library building directly impacts how the space should be designed.

Bennett's research explored the motivating factors guiding the 1990s renovations. The strongest motivating factor, cited by 57 percent of respondents, was the need to accommodate the growing print collection by expanding shelving or designing off-campus storage facilities. Bennett stated that this factor was an example of extrapolative planning exemplifying "traditional library services," which identified the building as a place where information is held. The second strongest motivator, cited by 45 percent of respondents, was the "changing characteristics of student study space needs" (2003, 7). Bennett argued that this motivator indicated a need to use interpolative planning as opposed to extrapolative planning in redesigning space. Interpolative planning involved focusing on "the uses of library space that cannot be simply predicted from past patterns of use" such as the users' need to create their own space for learning. The survey indicated how important it is for libraries to plan for what students may need in the future, needs that may divert resources from traditional library services.

Bennett's survey revealed that academic libraries were becoming interested in creating more space for the user. Library directors repeatedly commented on the need to focus more on the user, group study space, and the need for social spaces in the library. The demand for social spaces in the library, whether it be lounges, cafes, or outdoor seating, illustrated the need to accommodate the user and provide them an environment that they find conducive to their learning. Academic libraries experienced a shift focusing more on their users or learners and their need for space rather than on creating more space for the collection (Bennett 2009).

Demas and Scherer also address the importance of library space and its purpose in the community. In their article "Esprit de Place" (2002), Demas and Scherer state that libraries satisfy an important need for people to be a part of the community. They discuss various uses of space, how these contribute to building community and a sense of a place, and how transcendent and transportive spaces relate to the library building. Transcendent space extends beyond the brick walls of the building to educating the users about ideas and concepts relevant in the community. Transportive space in the library involves design that inspires patrons and enhances their unique experience while in the library. Through the use of transcendent and transportive spaces, libraries give the users the opportunity to connect with the library and community. Such spaces make the library a "serious, welcoming and enjoyable physical destination" (65).

In his book *The Great Good Place* (1999), sociologist Ray Oldenburg posited the concept of the "third place," a place where people choose to go that is outside of their work or home. When considering the role of the library building and the needs of the users, the library can become the "third place" giving them a place to meet and create a sense of community. At first glance, the phrase "third place" is not one American librarians may want to equate with their locus of professional practice. In America's competitive culture, "third place" often evokes an image of doing well enough to gain recognition, but not winning a competition. But Oldenburg's third place is relevant. According to Oldenburg, a "third place" provides people with the space to engage in conversation and build a sense of community. A third place offers a comfortable welcoming environment for informal gathering where people come and go at their leisure and nobody is "required to play host" (22). The relaxed atmosphere of the third place provides users with the chance to be around others where they are not restricted by time, nor are they compelled to be there. The comfortable setting of the third place provides users with a place to relax, feel at home, and be themselves.

The third place also gives people the opportunity to interact with others of different social ranks, philosophies, and interests. The allure of third places is not the beauty of the location, but rather other people in that place. People are stimulated by the fact that third places offer familiar faces but also satisfy their expectation of seeing new ones (Oldenburg 1999). The library as a third place provides faculty members and students a place to comfortably meet others from different economic or social backgrounds, different disciplines, and different areas of the academy. Demas and Scherer highlight the fact that transcendent spaces, like third places, "create opportunities for people who do not necessarily travel in the same disciplinary, social, political, or economic circles to frequently meet and greet each other" (2002, 65). Comfortable third places provide an inclusive environment giving users the opportunity to meet new people with new ideas. Those who spend time at third places also find comfort in seeing familiar strangers. These individuals may not interact, yet spending time at the third place provides a common bond and a familiarity in their relationship. Libraries are, and will continue to be, open spaces for all users to take advantage of and thus are naturally inclusive—third—places.

In these comfortable, welcoming environments, conversation is the main activity. People engage freely with each other discussing topics of interest.

In the third place, conversation is valued and the tone is playful and the "mood is light" (Oldenburg 1999). People participating in the discussion are expected to enhance it and not detract from it. Oldenburg states that the diverse makeup of the third place prevents a singular voice from dominating the dialogue. The conversation in a third place gives people the opportunity to share their experiences while learning from other people, and the social engagement that occurs in the third place evolves from that conversation. Thinking about the library as a third place recognizes that conversation contributes to the welcoming and comfortable atmosphere that users seek. Oldenburg is referring to spoken conversation between individuals, but in a very real sense the conversation can also include the scholarly communication through time as people engage with the library's information resources.

The relaxed atmosphere and open conversation of the third place satisfies the user's need for human connection. For many users, the third place provides the opportunity to meet with others and discuss topics of interest. They enjoy the conversation and socialization a third place offers along with the opportunity to interact with familiar faces and meet new ones. For other users, human connection involves being part of the group without necessarily being "in" the group. In many libraries, these users are interested in being around others but at the same time want to maintain their privacy. The social interaction available in libraries is an allure, but users can also choose to be alone in that academic space. Demas emphasizes that a popular draw of academic libraries "is the unique pleasure of being alone, in a quiet place, while simultaneously being in a public place associated with scholarship" (2005, 2).

People who frequent third places create community. The open conversation and relaxed atmosphere engage them and make them the focus of the third place. The conversations generated make them feel like it is their place—a place created for their use. The personal relationships that draw people to the third place, along with the relaxed atmosphere, develop a sense of community. Demas and Scherer state that because it draws people together, the library building is a "vital agent in community-building" (2002, 65). Bennett's study quoted one director regarding the academic library as a community space as stating, "'this is their [the students] community now. They've left home; this is their world'" (Bennett 2003, 24). The library as the third place creates a vibrant community, giving users the opportunity to be themselves and take advantage of what the library building provides.

NetGen students, millennials, or digital natives have caused a significant shift in the pedagogy delivered by professors in colleges and universities. College and university instruction now involves more discussion rather than lecture. The focus has shifted to the students engaging with information and with each other and away from the instructor simply providing the information. Learning has become more social and collaborative. In addition, there is greater recognition that much of the learning is occurring outside the classroom, in informal learning spaces where students are comfortable and feel welcomed.

Social learning emphasizes the role of the student in the learning process. As an integral part of the pedagogy, students work together to understand concepts and create knowledge. Brown and Adler define social learning as "based on the premise that our understanding of content is socially constructed through conversations about that content and through grounded interactions especially with others around problems or actions" (2008, 18). In this learning environment, students are expected to participate. They are expected to express their viewpoints and contribute to the conversation. Social learning requires students to have space to gather, converse, and share their knowledge outside the classroom, the dorm room, or home. The space students need has to be a third place where they feel comfortable and welcomed.

Colleges and universities must create third places for their students. According to Oldenburg, higher education administrators need to encourage conversation and learning outside the classroom (Oldenburg 1997). The campus library can provide students with a place for social learning and conversation. In Bennett's survey, library directors overwhelmingly argued for the importance of libraries providing space for the users to meet. One director stated that the library satisfies the "basic human need for comfortable space" (2003, 24). Demas and Scherer remarked that libraries as transportive spaces must include warmth and style in their design, making it an inviting place for the user. Giving students a third place allows them to create connections with each other. These connections create their community, which Oldenburg asserts contributes to personal growth. For a successful third place on campus, Oldenburg sets three parameters. They are that it must

- be easy to get to,
- provide food & drink, and
- have a design that invites students in and allows them to linger. (1997, 93)

Oldenburg stresses that third places, or hangouts, on campus contribute to learning by allowing students the opportunity to build community. Their community helps them grow and develop outside the classroom. In her article examining the role of the library and NetGen students, Lippincott states that "libraries can promote community by providing comfortable spaces for informal gatherings of students" (2005, 64). But the community in third places is not comprised exclusively of students. Faculty members are also users of third places. They can meet students in these informal learning and social environments, contribute to the conversation, and be active members of the third place community.

For many colleges and universities, the term community is central to their mission. At Rollins College, community is one of the three guiding principles in the college's mission statement (Rollins College 2009). While the focus of community at Rollins is engagement with the community, both global and local, beyond the campus, the concept of community creates a sense of belonging among students, giving them a common bond. In an analysis of mission statements of Canadian universities, researchers found that the value of community ranked fifth out of the twelve core values identified among various institutions (Kreber and Mhina 2007). Within the value of community, institutions emphasized cooperation and collaboration as the focus of community on their campus. The library as a third place provides users the space to learn from each other and build a community of learners. It demonstrates how academic libraries are advancing the mission of the academy by evolving into a place for active learning where students create their community.

As a part of their educational experience, the library as a third place creates among its users a fondness and attachment to that place. The users develop a sense of loyalty, inspiring them to return regularly while enrolled in the institution. More importantly, creating a third place community can evolve into a stronger connection among alumni to their alma mater (Young 2010). The qualities of the users who compose the third place community, making it their own, can extend beyond the present use and into future institutional support. Thus the library's role as a third place in the academic community can contribute to student success, student retention, and alumni support. It is important that academic administrators understand the contribution the library can play in these key institutional goals.

At Rollins' Olin Library, we have taken strides to develop the building into a third place on campus. We revised our mission statement to include the phrase, "a welcoming environment for the Rollins community" (Olin Library 2007). The library created a new librarian position whose role is to consciously think about the library as a third place. While one element within this is to reach out to the campus community and coordinate the displays and events, the most important task is to focus on the library as a third place and ensure that we remove as many impediments as possible to the users' taking control of the space to meet their own learning and social needs, while still maintaining exceptional information services and resources. We eliminated our food and drink policy and expanded the offerings and hours of a café at the center of the building. We transformed the main floor of the building into an area for open conversation and discussion. Students can meet classmates and discuss material or just chat with one another. Students can also meet in group study spaces located throughout the building. Often faculty members and students meet in the library and discuss issues or interests. Class and meeting rooms, bookable within the campus-wide events scheduling system, encourage students, faculty, and staff to view the library building as a convenient place to meet both formally and informally. We have been so successful that the students affectionately refer to the library as "Club Olin."

Knowing the student's need for a variety of spaces, the library maintains quiet and individual study spaces on separate floors. The challenge we face is to balance the desire for our users to feel welcomed and comfortable while at the same time fulfilling their need for a quiet library that inspires studying and learning. Our library staff members work hard not to be perceived as "the library police." The atmosphere in particular spaces and floors is self-regulated by the people using those spaces. We have also worked to develop partnerships with campus departments and become involved in student activities and events. The library has hosted film showings for the Global Peace Film Festival, election night parties, book discussion groups, and during orientation the entire building is given over to academic advising.

Through these partnerships, the library has dedicated exhibit space in the lobby to promote campus events and issues that are important or of interest to our users. Thus, while in many libraries displays and exhibits are designed to highlight the resources of the library (and, by implication, why someone might want to make more use of those resources), in the Olin Library we actively discourage the addition of books and other library materials to displays and exhibits. Books, unless they are rare or lavishly illustrated, are inherently uninteresting to look at. After all, Ranganathan, in his first law, did not say books are to look at. No, he stated, "books are for use" (Ranganathan 2006). By placing books in displays, often behind glass, and certainly not where users expect to find them, librarians make them less accessible than they might normally be. We also make the implicit statement to our users that the library is there to present materials and ideas to the user, instead of a place in which the library has control. Therefore, at the Olin Library, we seek opportunities to present student art work, class projects, student organization events and issues, and to link to the events and issues important to other elements of the college such as the Winter Park Institute, Winter With the Writers, the Cornell Fine Arts Museum, First Year Explorations, and the Office of Multicultural Affairs. This gives the Rollins community a sense that the library is their space, a space they control and within which they can expect to make statements and initiate conversations that are important to them and of interest to their fellow community members.

During the process of transforming our building into one centered on our users, like most college libraries in the "new normal," the library has not gained any additional funding for remodeling or renovation. Working with an external consultant, we streamlined our book ordering and processing work flow. The new process, combined with a number of staff retirements, provided an opportunity to reduce staff in our Technical Services Department. Those funds were reallocated, enabling the library to hire the new public services librarian mentioned above, with a focus on the user experience and the library's role as a third place. Even with that reallocation we have a lower total FTE (Full-time equivalent) than we had in 2006. That position and its focus on the user experience further demonstrate our commitment to our users and their experience in the library. In our partnership with other groups on campus, the library has seen nominal increases in its food and printing expenses in order to make the events successful. To date, Olin Library has taken intentional steps to reorient the building to serve the user's learning needs. We intend to continue investigating their needs through focus groups, surveys, or observation in order to make the library the "third place" on campus.

As college librarians, we must not let the fiscal constraints of the new normal restrict our imaginations as we seek to partner with our users in creating the college library of the twenty-first century. It is too easy to retreat into more traditional forms of librarianship in the face of tight budgets and reduced staffing. Instead, just as academic administrations are questioning many of the "sacred cows" of twentieth-century college life, we should also continue to investigate and question the role of the library as place in our users' lives. When we look at the library from our users' perspective, it is our contention that the development in the last decade of the user-centric library will turn out to be more valuable and contribute more to the bottom line of student success than some of our more traditional uses of space.

REFERENCES

Association of College and Research Libraries. 2010. Marketing @ your library. http://www.ala.org/ala/mgrps/divs/acrl/issues/marketing/index.cfm.

Bennett, S. 2003. Libraries designed for learning. Washington, DC: Council on Library and Information Resources. http://www.clir.org/pubs/reports/pub122/pub122web.pdf.

———. 2009. Libraries and learning: A history of paradigm change. *Portal: Libraries and the Academy* 9:181–97.

Brown, J. S., and R. P. Adler. 2008. Minds on fire: Open education, the long tail, and learning 2.0. *Educause Review* 43:17–32. http://foruminnova.files.wordpress.com/2007/12/minds_on_fire.pdf.

Cronin, B. 1982. New technology and marketing – the challenge for librarians. *ASLIB Proceedings* 34:377–93.

Davis, J. B. 1990. Assistance for victims and witnesses. *Orange Coast Magazine*, February, 168.

Demas, S. 2005. From the ashes of Alexandria: What's happening in the college library? In *Library as place: Rethinking roles, rethinking space*, 25–40. http://www.clir.org/pubs/reports/pub129/pub129.pdf.

Demas, S., and J. A. Scherer. 2002. Esprit de place. *American Libraries*, April, 65–68.

Edinger, J. A. 1980. Marketing library services: Strategy for survival. *College & Research Libraries* 41:328–32.

Fast Company. 2002. Idea fest. The new business conversation starts here. 23 bright ideas for a stellar 2003. http://www.fastcompany.com/magazine/66/ideafest.html.

Gwyn, R. 1992. Maybe this scary economy is the new normal. *Toronto Star*, August 2, B3.

Howard, J. 2009. In face of professors' "fury," Syracuse U. library will keep books on shelves. *The Chronicle of Higher Education*, November 12. http://chronicle.com/article/In-Face-of-Professors-Fur/49133/.

Ithaka. 2009. Chapter 1: Discovery and evolving role of the library. In *Faculty Survey 2009*. http://www.ithaka.org/ithaka-s-r/research/faculty-surveys-2000-2009/faculty-survey-2009.

Kreber, C., and C. Mhina. 2007. The values we prize: A comparative analysis of the mission statements of Canadian universities. *Higher Education Perspectives* 3:60–79. https://twpl.library.utoronto.ca/index.php/hep/article/viewFile/650/714.

Lippincott, J. K. 2005. Net Generation students and libraries. In *Educating the net generation*, ed. D. G. Oblinger and J. L. Oblinger. Boulder, CO: Educause. http://www.educause.edu/Resources/EducatingtheNetGeneration/NetGenerationStudentsandLibrar/6067.

Matthews, B. 2009. *Marketing today's academic library: A bold new approach to communicating with students*. Chicago: American Library Association.

Norman, O. G. 1989. Marketing library and information services: An annotated guide to recent trends and developments. *Reference Services Review* 17:43–64.

Oldenburg, R. 1997. Making college a great place to talk. In *The best of planning for higher education*, 90–94. http://eric.ed.gov/PDFS/ED472314.pdf.

———. 1999. *The great good place*. New York: Marlowe & Company.

Olin Library. 2007. Welcome to the Olin Library at Rollins College planning wiki. http://olinplan.pbworks.com/.

Ranganathan, S. R. 2006. *The five laws of library science*. New Delhi: Ess Ess Publications.

Rollins College. 2009. Mission statement. http://www.rollins.edu/why-rollins/mission.html.

Young, S. 2010. Looking beyond the stacks: The law library as place. *AALL Spectrum*, July, 16–21. http://www.aallnet.org/products/pub_sp1007.asp.

Strategically Leveraging Learning Space to Create Partnership Opportunities

TOMALEE DOAN and HAL KIRKWOOD
Purdue University Libraries, West Lafayette, Indiana, USA

The Management & Economics Library at Purdue University began a major physical and conceptual renovation four years ago. The conceptual renovation involves a rethinking of library faculty and staff roles and responsibilities based on the library's and university's strategic directives. The LearnLab space is being used as a springboard to create new partnerships, to implement our new roles, and to transform the perspective of an academic library's present capability. This article will highlight the variety of opportunities that have arisen by leveraging the LearnLab space.

INTRODUCTION

EDUCAUSE identified advancing innovation in teaching and learning with technology in an era of budget cuts as one of today's top teaching and learning challenges (Educause 2009). Jason Bearce, associate commissioner for higher education in Indiana, states, "every conversation we have with institutions now revolves around productivity. It's not enough to find efficiencies in their operations; they must seek academic efficiencies as well, graduating more students more quickly with more demonstrable skills" (Bearce 2010). Students today come to campus with varying levels of competencies and learning styles. Research findings show that unless a learner is engaged in actively constructing knowledge, little will be learned or retained. As research on the physiological aspects of learning has revealed, "Active engagement with the learning object—whether a lecture, laboratory process, text, or creative medium—increases the likelihood that the learner will both retain and be able to use information and skills later" (Lippincott 2009).

This case study will highlight the variety of opportunities that have arisen by leveraging the LearnLab space, a new instructional classroom space in the Management & Economics Library (MEL) at Purdue University. In the fall of 2009, the Management & Economics Library completed the first phase of a three-stage renovation. The first phase encompassed building a state of the art instructional LearnLab space and an adjacent quiet study room space. The funding for this project was provided through fundraising efforts and ultimately a donation from a Krannert School of Management alumnus together with a repair and rehabilitation grant (R&R program) awarded by the Provost office with the libraries matching the grant funds.

The R&R program was officially adopted by the Indiana State Legislature in 1981, and it employs a formula based on original cost of construction, building age, and the building's useful life. The goal of the R&R program is not only to preserve those buildings that are essential to daily operations as well as significant to the university's history, but also to enable Purdue to move forward, providing the best facilities and technology for our students and faculty. The award of a campus R&R grant for the phase one space sent an important campus message that the MEL renovation would allow Purdue to move forward with providing student learning spaces, leading to student success and allowing faculty to explore problem-based learning pedagogies in the LearnLab.

Until the completion of phase one, the vision for the library of the future had to be mostly articulated through architectural renderings and the actual sight of decreasing books and periodicals filling the collection-based space as they were relocated to a light archive browsable repository in the basement of the Krannert School of Management. MEL established a twice daily delivery service for patrons from the compact storage shelving space, while any item with circulation greater than twenty-two times remained in MEL. Removing low-use collections, retaining high-circulating items, and significantly reducing print reference materials whenever available electronically contributed to the move toward a total online desk top delivery environment. MEL encouraged students to use the library learning spaces by allowing food and drink into the library and brought in snack and drink vending machines through University Food Stores, a relationship useful for the phase three renovation, which includes a café. It is also important to keep in mind that building a state of the art learning lab facility won't necessarily mean it will be used in the way it was intended. Utilizing the space as a showcase was a primary objective as the LearnLab progressed toward completion.

The outcome of these strategies proved effective. Because we were able to drastically change the look of the library and deliver information needs to students, faculty, and researchers through new service methods, MEL began to gain significant understanding and support of the libraries' vision from the Krannert School of Management. The relationship between MEL and the Krannert School expanded in the areas of information technology, electronic resource collections, and information literacy instructional opportunities. It would be beneficial to describe the changed relationship. The school's advocacy for MEL and the value libraries can play in teaching and learning also increased. This initial interdepartmental relationship laid the foundation for all other campus success that has since occurred. The Krannert Dean asked the Library Head to speak to their Dean's Advisory Council during Alumni Weekend and provide a tour of the new LearnLab space. Every fall semester, Krannert has an executive lecture series with prominent business leaders speaking on hot topics in the field. As part of the speakers' visit, the school schedules a tour of the LearnLab space with the Associate Head of MEL promoting the instructional space as a key strategic initiative.

Phase one as a whole created an understanding of what a newly renovated library could accomplish in support of the school's and the university's strategic initiatives. Numerous faculty and administrators visited the LearnLab during construction. They perceived the space as innovative and became advocates for the libraries shifting paradigm. Some faculty members were early adopters and became instructors using the LearnLab for instruction after completion in the fall of 2009. In addition to the LearnLab's core purpose to promote engaging, technology-supported and interactive instruction, we are showcasing the space for fundraising within the libraries and within the School of Management by bringing in alumni and potential donors. As the faltering economy forces budget cuts, hiring freezes, and other cost saving measures, it is more critical than ever that professionals at all levels of the library organization contribute toward bringing in outside funding and developing strategic partnerships with campus units. This may not be in any past or current middle manager position descriptions, but it has become a necessity in today's economy.

SHOWCASING THE LEARNLAB FOR INFORMATION LITERACY

The LearnLab, designed by Steelcase Inc., is a forty-seat instructional lab (see Figure 1). It contains workstations, three multiprojection smartboards, portable dry-erase boards, and a digital copy-camera to capture information from the dry-erase boards. The layout of the lab promotes collaboration and communication; students face each other across several rows or pods of workstations. The chairs swivel and roll creating a space that can easily transition from individual work to team-based interactions and back again. The room has no true "front," thereby allowing the instructor to roam about the room, present from any of the smartboards, communicate more closely

FIGURE 1 Rendering for MEL LearnLab.

with the students, and connect the course content more effectively with the technology and the students.

The unique layout was attractive from the beginning, drawing in several School of Management MIS faculty interested in using it for their courses. This expression of interest, along with the HTM (Hospitality and Tourism Department) GS175 course, generated additional interest in the LearnLab from a variety of faculty. Activity in the lab has steadily increased and expanded over the course of the last year and one-half.

In 2009, at nearly the same time the LearnLab was completed, Purdue Libraries filled the newly created Wayne Booker Endowed Chair for Information Literacy. Information literacy is a key strategic effort for Purdue; filling this role brought campus-wide and international attention to the Purdue University Libraries information literacy initiative. The Purdue Libraries, in the years prior to the MEL phase one renovation, had begun to consolidate its campus spaces by eliminating and merging several libraries. A result of this consolidation was to bring the Hospitality and Tourism Department (HTM) into the purview of the Management & Economics Library. The norm had been one-shot library research sessions within selected courses in the HTM department; however, the department was revising its curriculum and saw a need for improved information research and literacy skills on the part of their students. The creation of the LearnLab and the hiring of a new librarian specifically to serve as liaison to the HTM department created a unique opportunity to meet the department's needs in information literacy. Librarians from MEL worked with faculty from the HTM Department to create a one-credit eight-week information strategies course that would be required for all incoming HTM freshmen. The MEL librarians have so far taught six sections of GS175 Information Strategies for Hospitality and Tourism. The eight-week format provided an opportunity to experiment and innovate with problem-based information literacy learning within the context of the LearnLab layout.

Preliminary assessment of students who have taken classes in the LearnLab has been extremely positive. Surveying over seventy-five students produced the following reaction to the LearnLab space:

- 91 percent felt that it was different from any class they have been in.
- 80 percent considered it an exciting room to learn in.
- 79 percent believed the room allows for more collaboration
- 89 percent considered it an environment conducive to learning
- 95 percent would like other courses in the LearnLab.

A representative comment from a student stated, "The learn lab is great. The technology is top of the line and I always check there first if I want to go to a computer lab, but usually it's full because everyone loves it. So maybe another one or two could be done?" We will assess the impact of the course over time as students move on through the HTM program to develop future strategies and information literacy initiatives. The creation of this course is opening the eyes of other departments and schools toward integrating information literacy and critical thinking instruction within their curricula. Increased interest is being generated from the School of Management, the Agricultural Economics Department, and the Consumer Sciences & Retailing Department to include an information literacy component within their programs. The MEL librarians are determining how best to scale our offerings to meet this demand.

The Management & Economics Library maintains control over the LearnLab scheduling; it is not part of the campus-wide classroom management handled by the registrar's office. The rationale behind this is twofold: first, the libraries want to maintain the multifunctionality of the space by allowing it to serve as an open computer lab when no classes are scheduled; and second, we have identified an important aspect that any faculty bringing their courses into the LearnLab must be willing to change their curriculum to take advantage of the layout and technology. The expectation is that they will experiment and teach differently; MEL Librarians vet all requests through this expectation. The accounting professor, a self-described non-techie instructor, was so enamored of the LearnLab that he completely revised his syllabus one week prior to the beginning of class to create a more dynamic, interactive course for his senior-level accounting students. An Associate Dean within the School of Management commented

> Instruction in business has long utilized teams and breakouts to compare perspectives, refine work product, better understand decision processes and hone consensus. Increasingly, this approach is not simply the dominion of management, but finds use in all the functional areas—economics, finance, accounting, operations, and marketing. A space like the LearnLab has given us a highly flexible but technologically structured overlay to conduct these class sessions. Through the computing technology, access to the information and computational power is ready and seamless; through the audio visual elements, brainstorming and work product can be shared with any granularity of the class. The physical layout allows easy instructor interaction with any team or team member, and rapid reconfiguring to groups as the learning goals warrant. Our faculty who teach in the LearnLab are invigorated by the capabilities and the students find the learning experience richer and more enjoyable.

The HTM professor was approved to bring in two of her classes, one sophomore-level and one senior-level course on business and e-commerce aspects related to the hospitality industry. A MEL librarian has been working closely with the professor to integrate information literacy throughout the course. They have conducted significant research on learning outcomes, and they will be presenting the results in a forthcoming article.

Interest in the LearnLab space was also high among other librarians within the Purdue Libraries. An information strategies course taught by a librarian from the Life Sciences Library focused on information literacy skills for Foods & Nutrition students. The course resulted from discussions with F&N faculty about how to better prepare students for the demands of upper-level courses. Most of the IL-related instruction occurred in the last two semesters of the curriculum but students needed it earlier and instructors wanted to have it emphasized and practiced throughout the curriculum. The course has been taught once thus far and is scheduled in the LearnLab for the spring semester 2011. Students in the first class found it to be a real asset, as did the faculty librarian. A geoinformatics course, EAS 591, has also been taught in the LearnLab. The instructor, Assistant Professor of Library Science Chris Miller, states,

> Geoinformatics provides a fuller picture of how one finds and evaluates information, prepares and manipulates data, uses the tools of analysis and visualization (including GIS), and conducts their work so that data and information can be made reusable by the next scientist down the line. A holistic perspective is presented in a hands-on, project- driven course with opportunities to develop various specific skills that collectively serve to ensure data is reusable by the greater scientific community.

The LearnLab enhanced his instruction and content; he continues, "A lot of the course content is intricate and procedural—GIS workflows, web service deconstruction, raw XML examination, etc.—and the ability to display and annotate this material in various ways was particularly helpful."

The LearnLab is also attracting activity for a variety of unique single event sessions including library-developed programs, such as the Competitive Intelligence Workshop for MBA students to School of Management Programs, the Experiential Learning Initiative, and cross-university wide programs like the Entrepreneurship Bootcamp for Veterans.

EXPOSURE

The phased renovation was necessary due to funding issues. We anticipated using each phase to build interest and attention for the subsequent phases to garner additional support and funding. The quiet study space and LearnLab were highlighted by the MEL librarians to a variety of groups including a prominent mention in the Krannert School of Management's Alumni Magazine in the fall of 2009 (http://earchives.lib.purdue.edu/u?/kmag,3453). The MEL Librarians gave demonstrations of the space to visiting librarians and administrators from Indiana University and the University of Notre Dame, the Libraries' Deans Advisory Council, a group of visiting Science Journalism Laureates, a group of visiting ARL Diversity Librarians, and to the university president and provost. This last demonstration resulted in the MEL LearnLab's being highlighted in the Purdue Alumni Magazine, *Collaborative Conversions* (http://www.pursuantgroup.net/purdue/alumnus/0310/default.asp?tpgid=10159438&sn=1r), and in the end of year message from the president as one of five key campus successes for the year 2009. This attention led to the university's student television channel visiting the LearnLab and highlighting it in one of its BoilerBytes segments on happenings around campus (http://www.youtube.com/watch?v = 3cb-fSbegQE). The BoilerByte segment was shown across the BigTen Network. This exposure, in turn, attracted visitors during the United States Agricultural Information Network (USAIN) Conference held at Purdue University in May of 2010, as well as librarians visiting during the Project Information Literacy Symposium held in October 2010.

The exposure the LearnLab received, whether planned by the MEL Librarians or by outside interests in highlighting the space, greatly facilitated development and support of phases two and three. Phase two consists of an adjoining space designed for team collaboration with movable tables, small break-out rooms, several group-work tables with LED screens, and a conference room. In 2010, additional R&R funding was made available across campus. The provost provided $250,000 for phase two, which was then matched by Libraries' funding. The generous approval of this funding showed that the Management & Economics Library was on the right path in renovating and redesigning our space and services. Phase two was completed and created an even clearer picture of the overall vision for creating student-centered spaces within the Libraries. Highlighting the two phases directly led to an opportunity with a donor to complete the renovation.

Fundraising efforts take careful planning, in-depth knowledge of the community, alumni, and university, as well as of library supporters who build and nurture long-term relationships with the library. It is most successful when everyone in the institution is supportive of these efforts and when joint efforts are made to cultivate potential donors. Creating a close relationship with the Development Officer within the libraries and also with the Krannert School of Management significantly increased the exposure of the LearnLab space and the opportunity to convey the libraries strategic vision to potential donors. Many tours, meetings, and instructional demonstrations were given by the head and associate head of MEL. One opportunity spurred a gift of two million dollars and a naming opportunity of a Krannert alumnus, Roland G. Parrish. A recent gift announcement for MEL stated that it would be renamed the Roland G. Parrish Library of Management and Economics, making it the first major Purdue facility to be named after an African American alumnus. The donor was passionate about the "experiences he remembered of the Library" during his college years that contributed to his successful business career. Library Dean James Mullins stated, "We are grateful for Roland's appreciation of our reconceptualization of Libraries spaces—from the traditional book-centered facility he remembered so fondly into a collaborative student learning environment" (Purdue Libraries Newsletter 2010). This gift will complete the final phase of the MEL renovation, which will complete construction in January, 2012.

LOOKING AHEAD

The LearnLab is now seen as a key learning environment that has received attention and praise by campus administrative leaders, including the president, provost, and Vice Provost for Academic Affairs and Student Success. This instructional classroom has been a catalyst for the academic community to gain a better understanding of the emerging role libraries contribute to learning and teaching. A few new campus initiatives are underway, including a task force to recommend a new model for university honors and student success programs, a task force to examine instructional equipment funds provided yearly to academic departments, and a course transformation initiative optimizing teaching for learning impacting up to thirty courses per semester over the next three years beginning in 2011. The Head Librarian of MEL has been asked to serve on these key initiatives representing the libraries' perspective about how learning spaces contribute to student success and retention and advancing faculty experimentation in the classroom. Without the demonstrated impact of the LearnLab, it is unlikely that the library would have been an invited player in these initiatives.

REFERENCES

Bearce, J. 2010. Putting a price on professors: A battle in Texas over whether academic value can be measured in dollars and cents. *Wall Street Journal*, October 23, C1.

EDUCAUSE. 2009. The EDUCAUSE top teaching and learning challenges. http://www.educause.edu/eli/Challenges.

Lippincott, J. K. 2009. Learning spaces: Involving faculty to improve pedagogy. *EDUCAUSE Review* 44, no. 2 (March/April): 16–25. http://www.educause.edu/EDUCAUSE+Review/ERVolume442009/EDUCAUSEReviewMagazineVolume44/163794.

Purdue University Libraries Newsletter 2010. Roland Parrish's $2 million gift puts Libraries on the fast track to the future. Fall, 1.

SELECTED RESOURCES IN LEARNING SPACES

Barton, E., and A. Weismantel. 2007. Creating collaborative technology rich workspaces in an academic library. *Reference Services Review* 35:395–404.

Beagle, D., D. R. Bailey, and B. Tierney. 2006. *The information commons handbook.* New York: Neal-Schuman.

Beard, J., and P. Dale. 2008. Redesigning services for the Net-Gen and beyond: A holistic review of pedagogy, resource, and learning space. *New Review of Academic Librarianship* 14:99–114.

Coffield, F., D. Moseley, E. Hall, and K. Ecclestone. 2004. *Learning styles and pedagogy in post-16 learning: A systematic and critical review.* London: Learning and Skills Research Centre. http://www.hull.ac.uk/php/edskas/learning%20styles.pdf.

Cook, D. 2000. Creating connections: A review of the literature. In *The collaborative imperative: Librarians and faculty working together in the information universe*, ed. R. Raspa and D. Ward, 19–38. Chicago: Association of College and Research Libraries.

Dewey, B. I. 2008. Social, intellectual, and cultural spaces: Creating compelling library environments for the digital age. *Journal of Library Administration* 48:85–94.

Doan, T., and M. L. Kennedy. 2009. Innovation, creativity, and meaning: Leading in the Information Age. *Journal of Business & Finance Librarianship* 14:348–58.

Haggis, T. 2009. What have we been thinking of? A critical overview of 40 years of student learning research in higher education. *Studies in Higher Education* 34:377–90.

Hunley, S., and M. Schaller. 2006. Assessing learning spaces. In *Learning Spaces*, ed. D. Oblinger. http://www.educause.edu/learningspacesch13.

Klusek, L., and J. Bornstein. 2006. Information literacy skills for business careers: Matching skills to the workplace. *Journal of Business & Finance Librarianship* 11:3–21.

Lippincott, J. K. 2006. Linking the information commons to learning. In *Learning spaces*, ed. D. G. Oblinger, 7.1–7.8. EDUCAUSE. http://www.educause.edu/learningspaces.

New Media Consortium. 2009. 2010 Horizon report preview. http://www.nmc.org/pdf/2010-Horizon-Report-Preview.pdf.

Oblinger, D. 2005. Leading the transition from classroom to learning spaces. *EDUCAUSE Quarterly* 28:14–18. http://www.educause.edu/EDUCAUSE± Quarterly/EQVolume282005/EDUCAUSEQuarterlyMagazineVolum/157336.

Powell, D. 2008. Evaluation and the pedagogy-space-technology framework. In *Learning spaces in higher education: Positive outcomes by design: Proceedings of the Next Generation Learning Spaces 2008 Colloquium*, ed. D. Radcliffe, H. Wilson, D. Powell, and B. Tibbetts, 25–30. Brisbane: University of Queensland. http://www.uq.edu.au/nextgenerationlearningspace/proceedings.

Radcliffe, D. 2008. A pedagogy-space-technology (PST) framework for designing and evaluating learning places. In *Learning spaces in higher education: Positive outcomes by design: Proceedings of the Next Generation Learning Spaces 2008 Colloquium*, ed. D. Radcliffe, H. Wilson, D. Powell, and B. Tibbetts, 9–16. Brisbane: University of Queensland. http://www.uq.edu.au/nextgenerationlearningspace/proceedings.

Roberts, S., and M. Weaver. 2006. Spaces for learners and learning: Evaluating the impact of technology-rich learning spaces. *New Review of Academic Librarianship* 12:95–110.

Savin-Badin, M. 2008. Learning spaces, agency and notions of improvement: What influences thinking and practices about teaching and learning in higher education? An interpretive meta-ethnography. *London Review of Education* 6:211–27.

Silver, H. 2007. Use of collaborative spaces in an academic library. PhD diss., Simmons College. http://dspace.mit.edu/handle/1721.1/38491.

Steelcase. n.d. LearnLab: A Steelcase research project. http://www.steelcase.com/en/Resources/industries/education/Documents/LearnLab%20A%20Steelcase%20Research%20Project.pdf.

Stuart, C. 2009. Learning and research spaces in ARL libraries: Snapshots of installations and experiments. *Research Library Issues: A Bimonthly Report from ARL, CNI, and SPARC* 264:7–18. http://vnweb.hwwilsonweb.com/hww/results/getResults.jhtml?_DARGS=/hww/results/results_common.jhtml.35

Weiner, S. A. 2009. The contribution of the library to the reputation of a university. *The Journal of Academic Librarianship* 35:3–13.

Hitching Your Wagon to the Right Star: A Case Study in Collaboration

LEA SUSAN ENGLE
Texas A&M University, College Station, Texas, USA

In tough economic times, librarians are challenged to increase their instruction and outreach efforts despite shrinking budgets. This article discusses creating a mutually beneficial partnership with existing, successful campus programs to increase outreach efforts with minimal financial risk. Ten steps for creating a meaningful partnership are discussed. The author uses lessons learned from her own experience creating a collaboration with a first-year orientation program to illustrate the challenges and suggest best practices to help readers implement the model on their own campuses.

INTRODUCTION

Today's academic librarians are challenged by two opposing factors: ever-shrinking budgets and an increased emphasis on outreach. Undergraduate and outreach librarians are forced to connect with their students with little or no money. At Texas A&M University, the undergraduate population is over 36,000 students, 8,000 of whom are first-year students. The library attends resource fairs, holds an open house, and offers tours for new students and their parents. While these events are well-attended, it is difficult for the library table to compete with other "more fun" and better-funded organizations like athletics, student activities, and Greek life. Students would rather visit the tables with free t-shirts and raffles for football season tickets than learn about the library.

In the spring of 2010, faced with an expanded outreach plan and armed with no budget, the author strategically selected the university's first-year orientation program as an efficient and cost-effective way of promoting the library to students. The potential impact is great, as over 70 percent of incoming students attend the orientation, which is lead by 1,100 upper-division students. Prior to 2010, the University Libraries had no official presence at Fish Camp. Through a clear letter of intent, networking, and persistence, the Learning and Outreach team was able to become a part of this unique orientation experience. This article first reviews pertinent literature to educate the reader on the key topics of university and library orientations and library anxiety. Next, a step-by-step model of seeking stellar programs and collaboration opportunities is discussed using examples of successes and missteps from the author's experience. The next section covers the implementation of the author's project and the results of the involvement. The last section discusses lessons learned and plans for improvements for upcoming years.

LITERATURE REVIEW

Although today's college students, often dubbed Millennials, are supposed to be more tech savvy and independent than their predecessors, they are not immune to the information literacy problems of previous generations. Despite their comfort with the Internet, Smart Phones, and a plethora of iThings, they still fall victim to library anxiety. Mellon first introduced the idea of library anxiety in 1986. Her qualitative survey of undergraduate students reported that "75 to 85 percent of the students in these courses described their initial response to library research in terms of fear or anxiety" and "most of the students who discussed their fear of the library talked about the feeling of being 'lost"' (1986, 162). Mellon and her colleagues implemented "warmth seminars" where students were introduced to library resources by a "warm, friendly, and approachable" librarian (164). Although these sessions did introduce students to academic resources like journals and reference materials, the main goal was to alleviate students' fear by providing a friendly face and helping them understand that their fears are completely normal. Six years later, Bostick expanded on Mellon's work and created the library anxiety scale, a measure that has been used in numerous quantitative studies of library anxiety (Bostick 1992; Brown et al. 2004; van Scoyoc 2003). Bostick's model allows libraries to uncover the kinds of library anxiety their users are experiencing by researching six different components: staff, resources, technology, reference, policies and procedures, and psychological factors (Brown et al. 2004, 4–5). For example, Mellon's warmth seminars may have touched on topics in each of Bostick's six components, but Mellon shifted the goal of the session from cognitive advancements, database skills, and card catalog/OPAC mastery, to affective changes. She wanted to change the way people felt about the library by providing them with the confidence necessary to ask for help when they need it.

Library anxiety prevents students from taking advantage of valuable library services, which can impede their academic success. While students may feel comfortable accessing electronic resources from home, library anxiety may prevent them from coming into the library and seeking help or even using online, interactive help features like virtual reference. While many students are able to find sufficient sources without seeking the help of a librarian, they are often searching inefficiently and not finding the best sources. Every student who has attended a bibliographic instruction session or a one-on-one research assistance session with the Learning and Outreach staff at Texas A&M in the past year has expressed that they learned things they didn't know previously, and the majority of students reported that they felt more confident in their library research abilities.

FIRST-YEAR STUDENT ORIENTATION

The literature on both university orientation programs and library orientations for first-year students is robust, but the literature on their point of intersection—library presence at university orientations—is relatively slim. First-year orientations have a positive impact on student success and retention (Blackburn 2010; David and Spain 2004; Tenofsky 2005). The library is a key to student success, and as orientation is closely tied with increasing retention rates, orientation leaders and libraries are natural allies. However, this seemingly obvious partnership can be difficult to form. Mills and Mitchell (2009) discuss their failed effort to incorporate the library into their university's official orientation program and how they created a competing program instead. Likewise, a team of librarians from the author's own institution discuss their difficulties gaining access to Texas A&M University's first-year-student orientation program (MacDonald, vanDuinkerken, and Stephens 2008). At Florida State University, two librarians were determined to promote their organization and its services at orientation "outside the walls of the library" as a "proactive way to market first impressions of the library outside the library facilities" (Rhoades and Hartsell 2008, 1). In her 2007 article on word-of-mouth marketing, Alire asserts that competition is a reality in today's academic libraries. Millennials are accustomed to getting instant answers from the Internet. Libraries are "no longer the only information service game in town" and because of this, "academic librarians can no longer sit in their ivory tower waiting for customers—students, faculty, and staff—to use their libraries. We no longer have a captive audience" (546). Like Rhoades and Hartsell, Tenofsky also believes that libraries need to be proactive and leave the confines of the library to "use existing [campus] groups" as venues for library marketing. Millet and Chamberlain (2007) agree that "tapping into student interests and groups is always a hurdle," but while it is time-consuming and work-intensive, "it never hurts to raise the visibility of librarians and market our resources" (98, 102).

Locating the standout program on your campus, one with a history of success, and preferably a solid funding source, can be challenging. Texas A&M University's fall 2010 enrollment was 49,129 students. On a campus of this size, there are dozens of student groups and orientation programs, and finding a program worth hitching your metaphorical wagon to is no easy task. Outlined below are ten steps for creating a successful partnership. These are a general framework, and there is room for flexibility. The steps ideally should be completed in order, but this may not be possible due to staff constraints, schedule conflicts, and institutional differences. Readers should be open to revisiting previous steps throughout the planning process.

1. Clear Statement of Purpose

The first step before starting any project is to know *why* you are doing it. Are you promoting a certain service like interlibrary loan or virtual reference? Do you want to teach a skill set like effective database searches using Boolean operators? Do you want to discuss the collection scope of an academic library and explain how it differs from public and high school libraries? All of these options are valid, and they are all examples of information relevant to the needs of first-year students. However, to successfully pitch the project to potential collaborators, one must write a clear statement of purpose with achievable goals. For this project, the author chose to follow Mellon's model of the "warmth seminar" (1986, 164). While wanting to engage the audience and use humor to help students feel at ease with the library, the author also slipped in a few of our best services to demonstrate how we can assist students both recreationally and academically. We sought to change students' perception of what a library is and make them feel comfortable approaching staff and the library buildings themselves.

2. Define Your Audience

Although the Learning and Outreach team at Texas A&M works with all students and faculty, the author's particular focus is on undergraduate students, with an emphasis on the first-year experience. In the fall of 2010, Texas A&M welcomed 8,176 first-year undergraduate students.

Focusing on just the first-year undergraduate students weeds out about 41,000 students; however, now our attention turns to the remaining 8,000. We needed to understand the process an incoming student goes through, and we began the way most Millennials would when faced with a research question, with the Internet, specifically the university Website. The author tried to replicate the experience of an incoming student, reviewing on-campus housing options, fraternities and sororities, service organizations, intramural sports and recreational opportunities, and orientation options.

3. Consider Your Options

From the list of student organizations and activities, the author narrowed in on two possibilities: residential life (on-campus housing), and our general first-year orientation program, Fish Camp. These seemed like the best choices because they were well-established programs that were utilized by the majority of the incoming class. Given that the author would be the only staff member focusing on this project and that a budget was nonexistent, getting the most for the least was my main objective.

4. Do Your Research!

After reviewing the organization's Websites and printed materials, it is time to do some talking. A resource fair is as much an opportunity for you to learn about the campus as it is for the students. If you're staffing a library table at a resources fair, go early, stop by the other tables, ask them the kinds of questions you wish people would ask you when they stop by to take their free library pen and shuffle past your informative brochures. Do not show your hand too soon. Do not approach a table full of strangers and tell them how you have this master plan to make their program better. Instead ask general questions like what do you want students to learn from your program, how many students attend each semester, what kind of advertising do you do, etc. This initial contact is not the time to pitch your master plan, but do promote library resources *as they relate to the organization's mission and goals*. For example, you may not want to pitch your new databases to a social group even though they may benefit the members, because their benefits and relevance may not be immediately and clearly apparent. Instead, you might emphasize your coffee shop or group study areas as places conducive to holding meetings or planning sessions. However, a discussion of databases and subject specialists would be an appropriate and relevant topic for leaders and residents in a dorm with an academic theme, like honors or engineering.

5. Make a Choice

This can be difficult, but remember to think about your users, their needs, and where they are. At Texas A&M, over 10,000 students live in dorms managed by the university's Residential Life office. Most of the students living in dorms are first-year students, but every dorm has both upper-division undergraduate and graduate advisors. Although the dorm population is greater than Fish Camp attendance, the more than one hundred dorms are not in a central location, thereby making it difficult for one librarian to get to all of or even most of the dorms. An additional hindrance is the lack of communal space in the dorms. The dorms at Texas A&M do not have large common rooms or computer labs. Most dorms have a small lounge that is a converted dorm room. These rooms can comfortably hold only between ten and fifteen people. Talking to 10,000 dorm residents, ten people at a time, in hopes of reaching the 8,000 first years was not an appealing prospect or an effective use of our time. Fish Camp won out because it was there where I had an opportunity like no other. At Fish Camp, one hundred miles away from campus and with no transportation, the students are truly a captive audience.

6. Make Contact

One of the most precarious steps is making initial contact in a tone that is persuasive, persistent, and patient, while not being pushy. Although you have created a plan, researched the organization, and been thinking about your projects for weeks, your ideas are new to your potential collaborators. Be careful not to overwhelm them, and remember, their programs are successful as is. They may be hesitant to incorporate any new material and organizations into an already successful model.

It is crucial that one understands the power structure before approaching an organization. Even if one has an existing contact with the organization, that person may not be the best person to contact. Libraries have an image problem. We are constantly fighting back against the outdated stereotype that we are a sterile and silent repository for books. We need to take responsibility for promoting ourselves in a way that aligns with the potential collaborator's goals. Handing off this duty to even an existing contact can be risky. Your enthusiasm and ability to speak clearly about your intentions for the program are your strongest asset.

7. Listen

Prove your worth by listening to student goals and needs. Instead of approaching the group with a list of improvements that you have been working on, use your first encounter to just listen. When you do speak, make sure to address them in their terms. You may be very excited about a new database the library just acquired, but if the potential collaborators cannot see immediately and clearly how that would benefit them, then save that information for another time or another outreach project. Although our ILL service (Get it For Me) is one of our best services in our library, pitching the newly renovated coffee shop would be better received because, as discussed above, the benefit of easy access to a coffee shop is apparent to a large audience and not dependent on their previous library experience. Remember that campus staff and faculty may also have library anxiety, so be careful to avoid library jargon and focus on services that show the library as welcoming and user-friendly.

8. Deliver

It is crucial that you make good on your promises. After working for weeks or months on integrating yourself into the organization or event and convincing them that your involvement will be beneficial, you need to make sure it does actually benefit the partner organization. The library representatives need to be prepared, enthusiastic, knowledgeable, and well-spoken.

9. Debrief

If formal assessment is not part of your plan, make sure to collect informal feedback from organizers and participants. Presenters and library staff should write at least one paragraph response to the event highlighting what went well and what was challenging. The library organizer needs to follow up with the event organizer to ask what worked and what can be improved.

10. Remember to Say Thank You!

It is imperative that you thank everyone who helped create your partnership. Leave a good impression by sending a handwritten note. This is also a good time to mention that you would like to continue your involvement in the event or organization.

PUTTING THE STEPS INTO ACTION

The author created a statement of purpose and researched the organization simultaneously. The two endeavors are mutually shaping, each continuously influencing the other, so that goals are influenced by the needs of the organization. Review the groups' main goals and learn as much about the programs as possible through their Websites, publications, library colleagues, and, most importantly, former and current students. Interactions with students tend to be the most informative. Our library employs hundreds of student workers, and they were very receptive to questions about Fish Camp. Some of them were Fish Camp counselors and provided insights from both sides of the Fish Camp experience. Their discussions of Fish Camp were frank and described how they felt about their experience, which was helpful when creating materials for the participants. Texas A&M's Fish Camp is the national model for extended first-year orientation. Each year 70 percent of incoming undergraduates attend sleep-away camp at an off-campus retreat center. Over four days they learn about the campus and its traditions and resources. They are divided into small discussion groups of twelve new students (Fish) and two upper-class counselors. Conversations range from academic resources, to which dorms and dining halls are best, to how to deal with a boyfriend who is attending another university. Strong bonds are formed in the groups, and counselors act as peer mentors and role models well beyond Fish Camp. Prior to 2010, the University Libraries had no official presence at Fish Camp. Through a clear letter of intent, networking, and persistence, the Learning and Outreach team was able to become a part of this unique orientation experience.

For new students, Fish Camp counselors are models of what it means to be a student at Texas A&M. Although all campuses have traditions, at Texas A&M tradition is sacred and akin to a religion. At Fish Camp students become Aggies. They learn the yells (cheers) they will use at sporting events for the next four years. Yelling is a key component of the Aggie experience. There are specific yells and traditions for each grade level, and the first-year-students learn theirs and practice it at least a dozen times each day. Fish Camp attendees are like sponges ready to absorb anything Aggie, and the library hopes that their involvement in Fish Camp will weave the library into the concept of an Aggie identity.

The groups are divided into teams branded with a team color and named after an accomplished member of the Aggie family who often visits the group during camp. The counselors wear their team color from head to toe for the duration of Fish Camp and often dye their hair the color of their camp. The students scramble to find clothing in their camp colors to mimic their counselors. A week of constant contact with each other, extensive practice of University, team, and class yells, and strong connections with one's camp team and color result in bonds that last well into the fall semester and often continue for the duration of students' time at A&M. Although the Fish Camp counselor is only contractually bound to adhere to the standards and regulations set by the Fish Camp organization for the year in which they are a counselor, the counselors are often thought of as an authority on all things Aggie and a trusted counselor far beyond their contract period.

It seemed that the best route to the new students would be through the Fish Camp counselors. The library's first official presence at Fish Camp began with eight back-to-back information sessions for the FC counselors. One thousand one hundred upper-class Fish Camp Counselors attended a presentation on library resources and were given a custom-made, twelve-page resource guide to assist them with library-related questions during their discussion groups. We learned from our Fish Camp liaison that the new students are very concerned with space—where to study, hang out, eat, etc. Questions regarding space are among the most frequently asked in the discussion groups. The resource guide directly addressed space questions and included basics like library hours, but also discussed the "feel" of the five different libraries—which were more conducive to quiet study and which areas were considered social space. The guide also highlighted five resources that the library does well that can help the students with their academic pursuits: our two kinds of resources guides, Get it For Me (our ILL service), Chat with a librarian, and the bibliographic management tool, RefWorks. These five resources are also highlighted in our instruction sessions for the first-year writing class. These sessions are attended by about 1,000 new students every fall.

Additionally, each of the over 5,800 Fish received a flyer that presented a picture of the library that correlates with the type of questions Fish Camp counselors are typically asked. This flyer and the twelve-page guide were copied and collated by the Fish Camp staff at no cost to the library. The flyer directed students to a corresponding Website that elaborated on the information, including links toward the highlighted resources. This flyer was in the students' welcome packet, with the library as the only academic department represented in the packet. The other materials were from student services such as Dining Services and Residential Life.

The one-page flyer highlighted the social aspects of the library and emphasized the library as a place to hang out, drink coffee, or use a computer. The flyer did mention our academic resources, stating that we have over four million books, but highlighting our popular materials like audiobooks, bestsellers and graphic novels in addition to our DVD and CD collection. The intent of the flyer aimed to showcase the services that students would not expect to find in a university library. The flyer included a link to a library Webpage created specifically for Fish Camp attendees, but accessible by anyone. A Fish-Camp-specific banner was displayed on the library Website to encourage Fish to visit the library's Fish Camp Website. The page reiterated and expanded upon the information on the one-page flyer and encouraged students to view a brief slideshow on the library's academic resources by enticing them with a drawing for an iPod Shuffle. To enter the raffle students had to respond to a question asking them which library resource they were most excited to try out. Although the site did not receive as many hits as we had hoped, we were still able to gain insight into first-year students' feelings about the library and its services.

The first year of Fish Camp involvement was a measured success. First, any positive interaction beats no involvement at all. Through counselor training, we had face-to-face contact with 1,100 students who were key influencers of our target population of first-year students. Additionally, we had indirect contact with the 5,800 Fish Camp attendees who received our flyer. While the Website was not very popular, those who did use it left positive feedback. Most indicated that they were excited about our ILL service, Get it For Me. The Website is a key part of the learning and outreach initiative as it ties the information presented at Fish Camp back to the on-campus resources and highlights academic services.

The most helpful part of the involvement with Fish Camp was the camp observation day. The author received special permission to make the one hundred-mile trek to the off-campus camp site and spent the day shadowing different teams, watching presentations by other campus organizations, and unobtrusively observing discussion groups. Fish Camp activities take place in about a dozen different meeting rooms. Each is decorated with team colors and symbols and large banners promoting campus organizations and traditions. The library was mentioned on a banner that appeared in multiple rooms. It didn't directly promote the library but included it on a list of important campus resources. This was the only official mention of the library outside of our flyer. Visiting Fish Camp was educational. One could see how the students reacted to the different kinds of presentations. Students were polite during the videos sent by some campus organizations that could not make the trip out to the camp site. Representatives who did make the trip up were greeted warmly and students engaged with the speakers—answering questions when asked, yelling at appropriate times, and applauding enthusiastically. Presenters who understood Aggie culture made in-jokes, and those who gave cues that sparked Aggie yells were the best received. Students also reacted well to the presenters who gave them free stuff.

This first year of involvement was a way to start what we hope is a long-term partnership with Fish Camp. We are making substantial revisions for our plan for Fish Camp 2011. Now that we understand the power structure, we can go directly to the new leadership to secure our role in the lineup for 2011. We are going to request a custom library banner for display in the Fish Camp meeting rooms. The Fish Camp counselors will make these with no cost to the library. The most important change for 2011 is that we will attempt to secure a spot on the on-site presenter list. This is not easily achieved, and each presenter must commit to attending each of the eight Fish Camp sessions, which requires a total of 1,600 miles of driving; although this is quite an undertaking, it is a one-of-a-kind experience and the best way to interact with a truly captive audience. Following Mellon's model of warmth seminars, the Fish Camp presentations would not be a crash course on all of the services in the library and demonstrations of database and catalog searches but an opportunity for students to have a face-to-face session, with a knowledgeable and enthusiastic representative of the library with the goal of reducing library anxiety and helping students feel welcome. Fish Camp has been successful for decades and it runs on a very tight schedule. We are counting on our success and the new relationship we cultivated with the Fish Camp leaders to propel us to the next step.

The biggest change for 2011 is that due to our success in 2010, we were able to secure library funds for Fish Camp. The Learning and Outreach team is devoting a significant portion of its budget to Fish Camp. Many of the giveaways that would traditionally be available at on-campus orientations and tabling sessions will now be available at Fish Camp. Comparable items will still be available at our on-campus tabling sessions as we do not want to alienate the 20 percent of incoming students who choose not to attend Fish Camp. The main difference between the Fish Camp and general promotional items is that the Fish Camp giveaways will prominently display the URL for the library's Fish Camp Website in an attempt to get more students engaged with the library Website. The Fish Camp giveaways will also be in team colors. Many of our general giveaways feature our school color, maroon, but Fish Camp teams are red, yellow, green, blue, purple, and aqua. For 2011 we will distribute Mardi Gras beads with a screen-printed disc. The disc will have a University logo and "Class of 2015" on one side and the library's Fish Camp site URL on the other. We anticipate students wearing the beads during Fish Camp and possibly attaching the beads or the disc to their backpacks when they get to campus. We intentionally did not use the library-specific logo on the disc as they can be easily removed from the beads. We felt that if the disc represented the students with their class year and had a general University logo, they would be more likely to keep the disc on the beads and become curious about the library Website.

REFLECTION AND CONCLUSIONS

Formal assessment is also part of the plan for 2011. This first year was about building relationships, getting our foot in the door, and learning the ins and outs of Fish Camp. The assessment of the 2010 initiative was qualitative, anecdotal, and based on one-on-one interactions with Fish Camp staff. Since we achieved our main goal of just getting the least bit of involvement, the project can be deemed a success. The anticipated increased Website traffic for 2011 coupled with more enticing raffle prizes will help us get feedback from more participants than the 2010 project.

Getting our foot in the door took years of casual efforts and six months of intense and focused work. Although the process was frustrating at times, after our first year of Fish Camp involvement, we are enthusiastic, pleased, and excited to continue our relationship. Hitching our star to the Fish Camp wagon is our best chance to reach the majority of the first-year students.

Although not every university has Fish Camp, every university has a successful program that engages students. Writing centers, student research programs, career centers, and tutoring programs are natural library allies. Libraries can also partner with Greek organizations and the athletics department, both of whom often require study hours for their members. Student services like residential life and dining services should not be overlooked. They are great venues for both passive advertising and outreach. In today's economy and environment of decreased budgets and increased expectations, starting a new program is difficult and risky. Instead, librarians should be encouraged to get out of the library and explore their campus for what they do well. By collaborating with successful programs, the library can increase its presence in a low-risk and potentially inexpensive way. The collaboration with Fish Camp cost the library less than $200 and potentially reached 70 percent of the incoming student population.

REFERENCES

Alire, C. A. 2007. Word-of-mouth marketing: Abandoning the academic library ivory tower. *New Library World* 108:545–51.

Blackburn, H. 2010. Shhh! No talking about retention in the library! *Education Libraries* 33:24–30.

Bostick, S. L. 1992. The development and validation of the library anxiety scale. PhD diss., Wayne State Univ., Detroit, MI.

Brown, A. G., S. Weingart, J. Johnson, and B. Dance. 2004. Librarians don't bite: Assessing library orientation for freshmen. *Reference Services Review* 32:394–403.

David, W. B., and J. W. Spain. 2004. Impact on freshmen retention of orientation course content: Proposed persistence model. *Journal of College Student Retention: Research, Theory & Practice* 5:305–23.

MacDonald, K. I., W. vanDuinkerken, and J. Stephens. 2008. It's all in the marketing: The impact of a virtual reference marketing campaign at Texas A&M University. *Reference & User Services Quarterly* 47:375–85.

Mellon, C. A. 1986. Library anxiety: A grounded theory and its development. *College & Research Libraries* 47:160–65.

Millet, M., and C. Chamberlain. 2007. Word-of-mouth marketing using peer tutors. *The Serials Librarian* 53:95–105.

Mills, M., and M. Mitchell. 2009. It takes a village to raise a tent: A case study in pitching the academic library to incoming undergraduate students. *Partnership: The Canadian Journal of Library & Information Practice & Research* 4:1–16.

Rhoades, J. G., Jr., and A. Hartsell. 2008. Marketing first impressions: Academic libraries creating partnerships and connections at new student orientations. *Library Philosophy & Practice* 10:1–11.

Tenofsky, D. 2005. Teaching to the whole student: Building best practices for collaboration between libraries and student services. *Research Strategies* 20:284–99.

van Scoyoc, A. M. 2003. Reducing library anxiety in first-year students. *Reference & User Services Quarterly* 42:329–41.

Delivering Information Literacy Instruction for a Joint International Program: An Innovative Collaboration Between Two Libraries

JISELLE MARIA ALLEYNE
La Horquetta, Arima, Trinidad & Tobago

DENYSE RODRIGUES
Mount Saint Vincent University, Halifax, Nova Scotia, Canada

This article focuses on a collaborative project between Mount Saint Vincent University Library and Bermuda College Library to introduce students to services and resources at the libraries of the partner institutions. Using Web conferencing software that allowed for voice, instant messaging chat, and live Web demonstration, a series of workshops was developed to introduce students to the concepts of information and literacy and reinforce for the students that they were able to access librarians and library services at both institutions. Issues relating to both the students' home library at Bermuda College in Hamilton, Bermuda and their remote library at Mount Saint Vincent University in Nova Scotia, Canada are examined, including the obstacles that have been surmounted as well as recommendations for other libraries considering this type of partnership. Strategies, activities, and tools used to implement the initiative are discussed.

INTRODUCTION

International partnerships are becoming prevalent in tertiary education. Agreements and memorandums of understanding are often reached at the higher administrative levels, filling the gaps in program offerings, and increasing enrollment in both institutions (Marshall et al. 2008). Students in these joint programs are often eligible for library services at both institutions. However, the literature is surprisingly sparse on the relationships within the libraries of institutions involved in these agreements, or on the access of students enrolled in joint programs to the library of the remote institution (Pival and Johnson 2004). This article presents an example of cooperation between Bermuda College and Mount Saint Vincent University in providing library instruction for students enrolled in joint programs at their institutions.

Bermuda College and Mount Saint Vincent University enjoy articulation agreements that allow students to begin programs in business administration, applied arts (child studies), and teacher certification at Bermuda College in Hamilton, Bermuda and complete their course of study at Mount Saint Vincent University (MSVU) in Halifax, Nova Scotia, Canada. While students for the past seven years have had access to the libraries at both institutions, students at the Bermuda College campus were less familiar with the resources available remotely to them at the MSVU library. Beginning in the 2008/2009 academic year, Web conferencing software was used to introduce library services available to students enrolled in these joint degree programs in Bermuda. These sessions focused on research skills and an orientation to online library resources.

This project of international collaboration in student library instruction contained the key elements of a successful partnership. First was the shared goal of providing quality research instruction to students enrolled in both institutions. Two librarians, one from each institution, led the project and both were involved in the selection of topics covered in the series. There were clearly defined roles and responsibilities regarding the scheduling of sessions, preparation of session materials, and booking of equipment and software. The venture enjoyed strong administrative support from program directors as well as chief library administrators. The project fit well with current instruction practices, and it further advanced the missions of both libraries.

LIBRARY INSTRUCTION BACKGROUND

The impetus for this exploratory study was an observation that there were no specialized instructional services for this specific user group, that is, students enrolled in joint programs at the institutions of Mount Saint Vincent University and Bermuda College. A second reason was to ensure that students upon transfer from Bermuda College to MSVU were equipped with the necessary skills to be successful in their sophomore years at the new institution. In addition, participants in the joint program were able to choose from all MSVU course offerings to complete their elective course requirements. This sometimes resulted in students choosing electives that were far more research intensive than their core programs, which were more oriented toward professional studies. Third, the collaborative project also emerged at the time of the expansion of Bermuda College's Distance Education program. Thus, the Director of External Programs and the librarians at both institutions saw this as an opportune time to collaborate. Most importantly, working in isolation was not in the best interest of the students, and this was the tipping point that pushed us to start this collaborative venture. Robert Hayes describes this as "the ethical commitment of librarianship to the concept of collaboration, that no library can be all encompassing and that sharing is the only way to ensure provision of access" (2003, 454).

The Bermuda College Library follows the traditional model of library instruction where students are brought to the library and are instructed in the access and use of library print and electronic resources. The Mount Saint Vincent University library had been attempting to provide library instruction for their distance students via DVDs distributed by the Distance Learning department, PDF instruction sheets linked on the library's Website, and through online flash tutorials. Despite these efforts, the Bermuda College librarian had heard anecdotal reports that students were unfamiliar with the library resources at MSVU and were having difficulty meeting their academic needs for MSVU courses with the Bermuda College library resources. At the same time, the librarian at Mount Saint Vincent University had received feedback from MSVU instructors that students in the joint program were less likely than other students to use library resources to complete their research assignments.

It was clear that in order for the students to grasp the depth of resources available to them for their courses in the joint program, both libraries need to work together. It was felt that using Web conferencing technology would be the best choice, combining the advantages of Web-based instruction with the benefits of face to face sessions, and promoting a virtual sense of connection between the two libraries. Howe and Strauss (2000) support this view when they reported, "library educators must adapt, and they must use technology, include the opportunity for social and interactive learning, and be visual and kinesthetic" (181). It would be the best means to help students acquire the necessary skills required for success in research-based course work. The sessions delivered through the joint initiative were based on the Five Session Library Instruction Model developed by Gandhi (2003), which showed that success is more likely if the information is packaged in short, focused segments.

LITERATURE REVIEW

Although there has been much written on the internationalization of tertiary education and the increase in memorandums of understanding among institutions (Altbach 2004), these accounts focus on the impact of these agreements at the wider organizational level rather than the experience of students or librarians studying and working within the context of joint programs. There has been a trend to partner institutions working together to enhance each other's offerings where there is little overlap in program content (Marshall et al. 2008). It is also relevant to note that the growth in these international arrangements has gone hand in hand with technology assisted learning that allows for distance learning (McLean and Dew 2006).

The *Standards for Distance Learning Library Services* issued by the Association of College and Research Libraries and the *Guidelines for Library Support of Distance and Distributed Learning in Canada* by the Canadian Library Association both endorse the concept that "when more than one institution is involved in the provision of a distance learning program, each is responsible for the provision of library materials to the students enrolled in its courses"(Association of College and Research Libraries 2008, 568). In the international context this has direct implications for library services at participating institutions, as the students' home library will likely not have the collections to fully support the joint programs, and students must access the partner institution's library remotely for their course research needs.

While much research has been carried out on the development and assessment of online library services to distance students, little research focuses specifically on programs offered through memorandums of understanding between institutions, and fewer still that speak to the issues involved in working with remote and home libraries. However, one such study that speaks to these issues was conducted by Pival and Johnson. They report that in a joint program through the University of Calgary, Athabasca University, and the University of Lethbridge, there were initially some difficulties in coordinating services among the institutions, but it was possible for three university libraries to support one program. They noted that "it can be challenging for students to learn how to interact with more than one library in terms of how to access different systems, resources, and support" (2004, 353). A common theme in many studies of services for distance students is that students accessing libraries remotely are often either unaware of, or do not make use of, the services available to them, often preferring to make use of geographically closer libraries (Buck, Islam, and Syrkin 2006; D'Angelo and Maid 2004; Slade 2004). In his overview of research done in the area of library services to distance students, Slade reports that the underutilization of library services points to a need for increased promotion and marketing, publicity, and library instruction, and that particularly when there is an international component, library instruction and information literacy training that is appropriate for the learning styles of students from other cultures should be provided (34-35). Buck, Islam, and Syrkin report that the technological emphasis in distance learning is particularly difficult for adult learners returning to higher education after years in the workforce, and that they are particularly vulnerable to library anxiety because many of them graduated in the early stages of the online era (2007, 1).

Additionally, in terms of collaboration within the area of information literacy instruction, much of the literature focuses on partnerships between librarians and instructors (Jacobson and Mackey 2007; Montiel-Overall 2007; Raspa and Ward 2000), or to a lesser extent on joint development of Web-based learning objects (Hansen 2001; Hansen and Lombardo 1997). While there is ample evidence that information literacy instruction is more effective when provided in the context of the course and linked with an assignment (Floyd, Colvin, and Bodur 2008; Jacobson and Mackey 2004), Owusu-Ansah (2003) makes the point that there are also inherent tensions in such relationships and not all faculty members are open to collaboration. While both librarians involved in this pilot project continue to work with faculty on other initiatives, it was felt that there was value in collaborating as librarians to provide information literacy training in their institutions' joint programs.

Regardless of the parties involved, there are lessons to be learned from the literature on partnerships and collaboration. Hooks et al. (2007) report that after a successful pilot project they needed to hire an additional librarian to maintain service levels generated by the collaborative projects with instructors. It was important to both libraries that sustainability and scalability be considered among the criteria for success of this project. Pival and Johnson note that clear lines of communication among collaborating partners are important if the needs of the students are to be fully met. They also state that "libraries considering similar collaborations need to avoid turf wars" (354). Crowther and Trott (2004) list the key elements to successful librarian collaborations as including the principles of shared goals and outcomes, defined responsibilities, strong administrative and technical support, and trust and respect (9).

METHODOLOGY

During the summer of 2008, the two librarians at both institutions communicated by e-mail to plan how they could work together to provide better services to the students enrolled in the Mount Saint Vincent University/Bermuda College joint programs. It was resolved that the sessions would be held in a computer lab at Bermuda College, with the MSVU librarian using Web conferencing software (which allowed for voice, instant messaging chat, and live Web demonstration) to provide remote instruction on the MSVU library-related research resources and services. As this software was used in many of the MSVU distance classes, many of the joint program students were already familiar with the platform. The Bermuda College librarian provided on-site expertise, ensured that everyone was able to accomplish the session tasks, and clarified questions asked when students appeared unsure of a particular point. Thus, it was reinforced that the students were able to access librarians and library services at both institutions for their courses. The students had access to a computer so that they were able to participate in practice sessions. While the Web conferencing software theoretically could have been used to reach students at their homes or workplaces, holding the sessions in a lab allowed for equal and supported access to the required technology.

As library research instruction is part of the regular duties of both librarians, these Web conference sessions were held as part of the regular work load and did not impose a cost on either organization. Heeding the advice of Pival and Johnson to reduce the barriers to communication between the collaborating partners, the Bermuda College librarian involved in the project was granted the status of "adjunct faculty" within the MSVU library. This allowed her to be provided with access to the MSVU library's electronic research resources and to better assist students with their research queries. Both librarians were fortunate to be well-supported by their institutions in arranging for the necessary equipment, space, and access to electronic resources.

The Director of External Programmes at Bermuda College promoted the sessions with the joint program students. The scheduling of the sessions took into consideration both full- and part-time students' schedules. In the 2008/2009 academic year, holding the sessions at lunch time allowed students engaged in full-time employment to attend. In the 2009/2010 academic year, the sessions were switched to evening. Students were asked to confirm their attendance and also to provide their program of study. This allowed the librarians to prepare examples and research scenarios that would be relevant to the students' areas of study.

In the fall term of 2008 one session was held, and it was called Introduction to Library Resources, focusing primarily on ensuring that students knew how to login to the library resources and how to access the electronic collections. In the feedback for this session and in the planning for the following semester, both librarians felt that there was a need to move beyond simple library orientation and move toward information literacy instruction. It was immediately apparent from the responses of the students that once the students knew where and what resources were available to them, they wanted to know how to use them more effectively for the purposes of their courses. In the winter term of 2009, four sessions were held, a repeat of Introduction to Library Resources and in the following weeks, Using RefWorks for Bibliographies, Using Google Scholar and Finding Quality Resources from the Internet, and Three Steps to Effective Journal Article Searching.

The session Using RefWorks for Bibliographies focused on combining proper citation practices with the use of RefWorks to assist in citation management and bibliography creation. Using Google Scholar and Finding Quality Resources from the Internet emphasized the critical evaluation of Web sources as well as how to check the MSVU library for access when proprietary journal articles appeared in Web search results. Three Steps to Effective Journal Article Searching focused on the development of search strategies, including the identification of research topics, generating keyword search terms, and the use of Boolean search techniques.

RESULTS OF THE COLLABORATION

In both years that the sessions were run, the attendance over the five sessions was about 10 percent of seventy eligible participants. While the overall attendance was low, most of the students who participated chose to attend all five workshops; their feedback was positive. All sessions were recorded and links to view them were sent to students who had not been able to attend the lab sessions. Both librarians were pleased with the outcome of the sessions because despite low attendance, we felt we had made a contribution to improving the services offered to students enrolled in distance programs. In a March 2009 e-mail memo to the authors, Peggy Watts, Director of Continuing Education and Distance Services at MSVU, stated that complaints previously received from faculty and students about access to library services for the Bermuda joint program cohort seem to have been resolved. In addition, as a direct result of this collaboration, we saw a fundamental shift in the way both libraries communicated with each other, resulting in benefit to the students. Although no formal posttests have been conducted with the students, instructors at Mount Saint Vincent have reported an increase in the use of library resources in course work over the two years that the instructional series has been offered. As only about 10 percent of eligible students are attending the sessions, it is assumed that there is some level of informal sharing of information taking place among the joint program students. More formal testing and research needs to be conducted in this area.

One advantage of the physical presence of the Bermuda College librarian in the sessions was that she was able to notice students' body language and to check their progress with the practice exercises. Several times in each session a particular step needed to be clarified or a pause was needed for all students to catch up. Having a MSVU librarian run the demonstrations allowed the students to make the acquaintance of the remote librarian. In the weeks following the sessions, both libraries were contacted about the use of resources for students' assignments. It was clear that students were moving from simply finding and accessing resources to using the tools available to them to effectively meet their information needs.

In the second year, the series sessions were also open to all Mount students who could attend the session virtually. As the focus of the sessions is for the joint program students, little promotion was done with other students beyond posting notices to the MSVU Library news feed on the Website.

Nevertheless between one and three students attended each session, and the interaction went well. While the focus of these sessions will always be on meeting the needs of the joint program students, this was an attempt to allow for more connection among the students of both campuses. It was part of the plan to move these sessions from the status of pilot project to the normal provision of information literacy session; thus, in the second year, more librarians from the MSVU library were involved in the instruction of the session, although coordination and communication with Bermuda College remained with the original project lead.

EVALUATION OF PILOT PROJECT

The success of this project was based on critical elements: first, the mutual respect and trust both librarians displayed toward each other. Allen and Hirshon argue that in order to achieve their goals collaborating libraries "must have a high degree of respect for, and deep seated recognition of, the value of increased collaboration" (1998, 43). Before and throughout the duration of the pilot project, both librarians had never met, yet still they maximized the expertise of each other, freely communicating and sharing information as well as providing on the spot training in the use of the technology where it was required. This reciprocity was key in bringing about a successful relationship and a successful project. This respect was also magnified despite the differences in sizes of the institutions involved. MSVU is a larger institution with greater technological resources, which could have created an imbalance, with Bermuda College not having a say in the direction of the project. However, this never materialized, and despite the various capacities to deliver instruction on e-learning platforms, both institutions were able to enhance each other's capabilities. As a result, both students and institutions benefited. An example of this spirit of cooperation was the awarding of MSVU adjunct faculty status to the Bermuda College librarian. This allowed the librarian full access to the resources used by the students in the joint program and allowed both institutions to be equal partners in the instructional sessions.

The second element that ensured the success of the project was the method of delivery chosen. Following the model developed by Gandhi by having the project span five compact sessions, it was possible to maintain the interest and enthusiasm of the students. Gandhi's model also proposed that the "instruction session be kept simple to cater to students with various technical abilities" (15). Since the delivery of the sessions was kept simple, all students were able to fully participate in a nonthreatening environment.

The ultimate reason for the project's success was that it filled a need and placed the students on a much more solid foundation. While it has been discussed that there are various kinds of library collaborations, it was felt that this type of collaboration filled a gap in the library literature and so fueled the determination to continue the project.

In addition to the benefits experienced by both institutions, Bermuda College also felt that as a community college this was the direction they wanted to take to enhance their teaching. Bermuda College saw this pilot project to be the model to be used in similar arrangements for articulation agreements that allow their students to use remote libraries in addition to their home library.

Looking to the future, there are several recommendations to increase the effectiveness of the workshops:

- More Effective Marketing Strategies
  We believe that by expanding marketing strategy, capitalizing on the technology, for example, using e-mails and texts, as well taking a closer look at the placement of the sessions, we will get a greater number of students attending.
- More Stringent Quantification and Measurements—Pre & Post Tests
  We believe that it is important to measure our success. As we go forward, we need to include measurements such as pre- and postinterviews, surveys, and learning style inventory tests.

CONCLUSION

The activity of libraries collaborating to enhance distance delivery services is one that should be encouraged, and especially in relation to international library collaboration this must be further explored. Both libraries are constrained by limited resources, but together they were able to achieve a higher level of support for their students than would have been possible alone. In the words of Finnerty, this collaboration has "proven that the belief in collaboration is a continuing force in libraries and the environment is ripe to foster this growth" (2004, 11).

REFERENCES

Allen, B. M., and A. Hirshon. 1998. Hanging together to avoid hanging separately: Opportunities for academic libraries and consortia. *Information Technology and Libraries* 17:36–44.

Altbach, P. G. 2004. Globalisation and the university: Myths and realities in an unequal world. *Tertiary Education and Management* 10:3–25.

Association of College and Research Libraries, Distance Learning Section, Guidelines Committee. 2008. ACRL's standards for distance learning library services. *College & Research Libraries* 69:558–69.

Buck, S., R. Islam, and D. Syrkin. 2006. Collaboration for distance information literacy instruction. *Journal of Library Administration* 45:63–79.

Canadian Library Association. Guidelines for library support of distance and distributed learning in Canada. 2000. http://www.cla.ca/AM/Template.cfm?Section=Position_Statements&Template=/CM/ContentDisplay.cfm&ContentID=3794

Crowther, J. L., and B. Trott. 2004. *Partnering with purpose: A guide to strategic partnership development for libraries and other organizations.* Westport, CT: Libraries Unlimited.

D'Angelo, B. J., and B. M. Maid. 2004. Beyond instruction: Integrating library service in support of information literacy. *Internet Reference Services Quarterly* 9:55–63.

Finnerty, C. 2005. An exploratory study of collaboration in New Zealand tertiary libraries. *Australian Academic & Research Libraries* 36:228–39.

Floyd, D. M., G. Colvin, and Y. Bodur. 2008. A faculty–librarian collaboration for developing information literacy skills among preservice teachers. *Teaching and Teacher Education* 24:368–76.

Gandhi, S. 2005. Faculty-librarian collaboration to assess the effectiveness of a five-session library instruction model. *Community & Junior College Libraries* 12:15–48.

Hansen, C. 2001. The internet navigator: An online internet course for distance learners. *Library Trends* 50:58–72. http://www.ideals.uiuc.edu/handle/2142/8383.

Hansen, C., and N. Lombardo. 1997. Toward the virtual university: Collaborative development of a web-based course. *Research Strategies* 15:68–79.

Hayes, R. M. 2003. Cooperative game theoretic models for decision-making in contexts of library cooperation. *Library Trends* 51:441–61. http://www.ideals.uiuc.edu/handle/2142/8481.

Hooks, J., C. Rahkonen, C. Clouser, K. Heider, and R. Fowler. 2007. Information literacy for branch campuses and branch libraries. *Library Philosophy and Practice (e-Journal)*:147. http://www.webpages.uidaho.edu/~mbolin/hooks.htm.

Howe, N., and W. Strauss. 2000. *Millennials Rising: The next great generation.* New York: Vintage Books.

Jacobson, T., and T. P. Mackey, eds. 2007. *Information literacy collaborations that work.* New York: Neal-Schuman.

Marshall, S., E. Brandon, M. Thomas, A. Kanwar, and T. Lyngra, eds. 2008. *Perspectives on distance education: Foreign providers in the Caribbean: Pillagers or preceptors?* Vancouver, BC: Commonwealth of Learning. http://www.col.org/resources/publications/monographs/perspectives/Pages/2008-foreignProviders.aspx.

McLean, E., and S. H. Dew. 2006. Providing library instruction to distance learning students in the 21st century. *Journal of Library Administration* 45:315–37.

Montiel-Overall, P. 2007. Research on teacher and librarian collaboration: An examination of underlying structures of models. *Library and Information Science Research* 29:277–92.

Owusu-Ansah, E. K. 2003. Information literacy and the academic library: A critical look at a concept and the controversies surrounding it. *The Journal of Academic Librarianship* 29:219–30.

Pival, P. R., and K. Johnson. 2004. Tri-institutional library support: A lesson in forced collaboration. *Journal of Library Administration* 41:345–54.

Raspa, R., and D. Ward. 2000. *The collaborative imperative: Librarians and faculty working together in the information universe.* Chicago: Association of College & Research Libraries.

Slade, A. L. 2004. Research on library services for distance learning. *Journal of Library & Information Services in Distance Learning* 1:5–43.

Building a Shared Digital Collection: The Experience of the Cooperating Libraries in Consortium

DORA WAGNER
Northwestern College, St. Paul, Minnesota, USA

KENT GERBER
Bethel University, St. Paul, Minnesota, USA

Recognizing the digital opportunities available, the libraries of eight educational institutions in Minnesota built on a previously existing consortial relationship in order to explore the possibility of sharing a Digital Asset Management System (DAMS). This article discusses the experience of these institutions as they chose CONTENTdm and the considerations made when settling on an option viable for a consortium. It elaborates on the shared cost considerations, hardware purchases, and the consortium's experience as it purchased and implemented the software, formalized avenues of communication, and established collection standards. We close by discussing the opportunities, challenges, and rewards experienced by those involved.

INTRODUCTION

The Association of College and Research Libraries' (ACRL) Research Planning and Review Committee's 2010 report (ACRL) includes the conflicting trends of increased opportunity for libraries to pursue new roles and services for their institutions at the same time that their budgets remain in stasis, at best, and dwindle, at worst. In the past ten years, digital libraries and digital collections have emerged as one of the main vehicles of opportunity. Due to the maturation of digital asset management software (DAMS) and increased interest in the concept of knowledge management, which is concerned with storing and providing access to local intellectual resources, many libraries have started to explore how these tools might augment and improve their services (Branin 2004). Until recently, smaller schools have lacked the resources needed to provide these services. As a result, larger institutions have led the way in digital collections (Markey et al. 2008). The resources necessary to support these kinds of services are large and require smaller intuitions to depend on shared efforts, demonstrated by other consortia such as Liberal Arts Scholarly Repository (LASR), HELIN, or state consortia like OhioLink and Consortium of Academic and Research Libraries in Illinois (CARLI), to implement and maintain them (Byrd 2010; Nolan and Costanza 2006; Xia and Opperman 2010). Thus, as the opportunities to reach beyond one's local library community multiply and the digital technologies available continue to improve, directors and their staffs are looking for creative ways to collaborate with other like-minded institutions in order to offer enhanced services while maximizing the impact of their limited budgets.

Recognizing the digital opportunities available, the libraries of eight private colleges and universities in Saint Paul and Minneapolis, Minnesota, Cooperating Libraries in Consortium (CLIC), discussed the implications of jointly purchasing and supporting digital collection management software.

The appendix contains school characteristics using the Carnegie system for classifying institutions of higher education. This discussion included what this shared relationship might look like and what the benefits to their home institutions might be, together with each institution's respective responsibilities and costs. It was the belief of those involved in the initial stages of this process that, as Murray (2010) states in *Toward Collaboration*, "collaboration will increase the strength of the library community."

The consortium pursued this opportunity because it identified the following benefits:

1. The ability to share the costs involved with the components of the digital asset management system (DAMS) makes this opportunity viable.
2. The knowledge sharing relationship among the members of the consortium maximizes the implementation and use of the DAMS.
3. The implementation of the DAMS expanded the capacity of each institution to serve its faculty, staff, students, researchers, and communities through the enhanced preservation, organization, and access to their digital resources.
4. This new endeavor supports the libraries' collaborative and innovative reputation both within and beyond their campuses.

In addition to the strategic and economic benefits, this article discusses the experience of these institutions as they chose CONTENTdm as their DAMS and what invested institutions considered when settling on a consortially viable option. It elaborates on the shared cost considerations as well as how necessary hardware purchases are supported, and it discusses the consortium's experience as they purchased and implemented the software, formalized avenues of communication, and established collection standards. The article closes by discussing the opportunities, challenges, and rewards experienced from this venture.

DIGITAL ASSET MANAGEMENT SYSTEMS

Digital asset management systems are a subset of content management systems (CMS), which are a collection of "tools, methods and processes to develop, implement and evaluate the management of content intended mainly for human comprehension" (Khosrow-Pour 2005). Usually related to creating and maintaining a Website, CMSs are already highly utilized by the business community. DAMS are a special kind of content management system that stores and indexes digital assets to facilitate easy searching, retrieval, and reuse. It also manages rights associated with those assets. The enthusiasm the business sector feels for DAMS has trickled down to colleges and universities by way of the library. In particular, DAMS are growing in popularity among educational institutions as a means to use their existing resources in new ways to provide increased access and to improve intellectual control over their archives or scholarly publications. Their popularity is due to the fact that a DAMS is "a set of processes that facilitate the search, retrieval and storage of digital assets from an archive" (Khosrow-Pour 2005, 869). As a subset of CMS's, DAMS excel in storing, organizing, and making digital content of a multimedia or visual nature accessible to users for repeated use without having to recreate that resource every time it is needed.

ASSESSING VALUE OF THE LIBRARY AND DAMS—LAYING THE FOUNDATION

Identifying items of value involves a knowledge of the institution's strengths and a level of communication significant enough to produce collaborative efforts. Different institutions will have different academic departments or offices that are best prepared to partner with the library in the creation of valuable collections. For example, Bethel library has a close relationship with its Archives and the Alumni and Parent Relations office. The Alumni board funds the student newspaper collection, which the Archivist and Digital Library Manager maintain. This partnership improves access to archival newspapers while also taking a step to preserve the materials since the actual papers are no longer handled by researchers on a regular basis; this represents but one example of how one department's funds and one's expertise can capitalize on a DAMS. Additionally, several institutions make the most of a DAMS strength in displaying digital images by collaborating on collections with art department faculty and students. Another example of campus collaboration is Northwestern College's theater program and poster collection, a comprehensive retrospective of the department's performances over more than fifty years of its existence. A recent study of the content in repositories of smaller masters and bachelors granting institutions shows that the largest two types of material collected are student work, composing 43.8% of the collections, and the Archives/Special Collections Department, with 19.3% (Xia and Opperman 2010). CLIC's collections consist mostly of Archival/Special Collections materials.

It is, however, worth noting that technology is not valuable in and of itself. Technology serves only as a tool by which organizations can enhance, extend, and amplify the existing quality of their own resources and services (Collins 2001). No institution should pursue a new initiative merely because a possibility presents itself, especially when each dollar of the annual budget is a vital piece in providing timely resources of high quality. In other words, a DAMS is not worth pursuing for the sake of chasing a trend. Rather, it is only as valuable as the resources it makes available and its subsequent utilization by invested institutions. It was, then, first and foremost in the process of purchasing and establishing a consortial collection utilizing a DAMS that the member institutions thoroughly explored their shared mission, the missions of each individual institution, and the institutional buy-in before pursuing the opportunity. Member institutions wanted to be certain that there was adequate staff to handle the responsibilities involved with creating and maintaining a digital collection as well as know that there was campus buy-in for these new projects.

When determining the value of a digital initiative, such as the one pursued by this consortium, it is imperative that the decision-making group outline a clear set of evaluative criteria by which to determine the need of a new program. The American Library Association points out that "it is important to pay attention to the trends around us to inform our thinking about where institutions of higher education and their libraries are headed," as this awareness will guide the way to intelligent decision making by involved parties (2007, 1). Tight budgets and the subsequent pressure on internal resources represent two of several factors that make assessment and demonstration of value an essential part of any library's service plan.

One such criterion is found in *Prioritizing Academic Programs and Services* by Dickeson (2010), which is written from the perspective of those who make budget and resource allocation decisions. Its premise is that higher education must make hard decisions that may involve taking resources from one area in order that another may grow. Many institutions adopted his suggestions, and this discussion of prioritization has become even more relevant with the current economic conditions and the release of an updated listing in 2010 (Lederman). Applying these criteria can help a program to thoughtfully advocate for the implementation of a DAMS or wisely refrain from pursuing the opportunity until a more appropriate time. The eight private colleges and universities in CLIC included the following of Dickeson's criteria when representatives met to discuss a DAMS:

1. History, development, and expectations of the program
2. External demand for the program
3. Internal demand for the program
4. Costs and other expenses associated with the program
5. Impact, justification and overall essentiality of the program. (2010, 66)

Understanding that administrators will be looking for these pieces of information, the Digitization Interest Group (DIG) focused its inquiry and assessment on demonstrating the program's relationship to these criteria.

HISTORY, DEVELOPMENT, AND EXPECTATIONS OF THE PROGRAM

CLIC online mission statements emphasize their long history of cooperation: "Cooperating Libraries in Consortium (CLIC) (http://clic.edu/) is a non-profit federation of the libraries of eight private colleges and universities in Saint Paul and Minneapolis, Minnesota. Incorporated by the college presidents in 1969, CLIC continuously works to improve library resources and services through cooperative efforts" (2009). Each of the eight participating schools is represented by their libraries' director on the CLIC Board, which also includes a CLIC executive director. While each of the individual institutions has a unique mission, the board functions under a shared list of goals. CLIC's goals served as a guide for the ensuing DAMS conversation:

- Provide improved and more comprehensive library resources and services to library users through the enhanced sharing of materials.
- Operate and manage an integrated, automated library system.
- Develop entrepreneurial initiatives in order to deliver new or expanding content and services.
- Provide opportunities for staff collegiality, leadership, and training.

In addition to relating to several key aspects of the consortium's mission, the (DIG) also cited several other key reasons why they believed that a digital program would benefit CLIC and its community.

First, "large amounts of data are created and stored- and must be found" (Khosrow-Pour 2005, 864). There is a demand, both by internal users and visiting researchers, for the information created, collected, and made accessible by the CLIC institutions. These institutions continue to amass historical and academic work for which the institution must create and maintain intellectual control. Historical documents, the papers of founders, the photos and periodicals capturing student life across the decades, and the academic work of the student body serve as valuable testaments to the school and its academic heritage.

While doing the best that they could with the means available, information professionals at each of these institutions felt that there was a more efficient and user-friendly means available. Information professionals take pride in their ability to collect, organize, and make accessible valuable information. These representatives felt, however, that they were not fully utilizing the tools available, and they intended to determine whether a DAMS was the means by which to offer "new pathways to help ensure the survival of the materials in these collections" (Lynch 2009, 2).

Many DIG representatives provided anecdotes concerning a challenging reference interview that would have been worlds easier had there been more thorough intellectual control of collections. Wistful smiles appeared on more than one face at the thought of being able to display a whole series of photos by subject, date, or artist without having to recreate the collection. Others were thrilled with the idea of sharing valuable information with researchers, giddy at the idea of being able to "extend library collections to include rich media data developed both on and off campus, and to make these collections readily available to faculty members, researchers, and students" (McCord 2002, 3). Since one of the core values of our libraries was to provide service, and our purpose is to collect and provide access of superior quality to our patrons, purchasing a DAMS was an opportunity to embody this "value and purpose" in a tangible way.

In other words, while library values are commendable, the institutions had to move forward in utilizing innovative technologies. Having these values while not acting on them is pointless. Information professionals are perfectly poised to provide their campus with the services a DAMS provides. Schools were interested in utilizing this opportunity and were further persuaded to move on the purchase of a DAMS when there was a consortium-wide interest. As an added benefit, moving together as a group of institutions provided a network of monetary and intellectual support that a single effort would not afford. The committee concluded that this digital platform would not only facilitate the organization of materials, but it would also transition directly into improved customer service and increased use.

The implementation of a DAMS would not only serve information seekers, it would also be a catalyst for cross-discipline or departmental collaboration. While in the planning stage this benefit was merely conceptual, after implementation the collaboration became a reality. Several of the schools can attest to the opportunity this platform provides. Marketing and communications departments are utilizing the system, as are art departments and history professors. There are numerous possibilities available to campus users, and although each campus may utilize the DAMS differently, each utilization has a shared result—the library enhances its image as an on campus information resource by facilitating the access and intellectual control of valuable institutional resources. The benefits of this symbiotic relationship are numerous, but, most importantly, "a library uniquely suited to its community can be the beginning of a virtuous cycle; the library reflects its understanding of the community; the community gets what it wants from the library and supports it" (Dempsey 2010, 23). What follows is only one local example of the energized conversations happening on campuses due to the DAMS implementation.

Bethel University is now digitizing the school's student newspaper and making it available through its Digital Library by using DAMS. One example of increased visibility and community participation connected with this project involves Martin Luther King, Jr. and whether or not he ever came to campus, as advertised in the school newspaper in 1960. Several interested parties consulted Bethel's archives as well as several other collections of Martin Luther King, Jr.'s papers at Stanford University and Boston University. After this investigation, documentation was discovered confirming that Bethel's president had invited Dr. King to speak and the invitation was accepted. It also revealed that Dr. King had to cancel his visit due to Atlanta's escalating student sit-in movement in late November of that year. This finding and exercise in primary source research was ultimately disappointing in that Dr. King did not, in fact, visit the institution; however, the campus has been encouraged and energized around the issue of Bethel's historical efforts to engage in racial justice, which has stimulated a renewed interest in this kind of internally focused research.

Choosing to implement a new program, especially in a time of financial challenge, is frightening. However, consortium representatives felt that the benefits of implementing a DAMS, especially as a shared responsibility and learning experience, outweighed the risks. This project would not only guard against stagnation but continue to propel the institutions forward, regardless of fears the current economy might breed. The goal of the DIG was to move forward thoughtfully as good stewards of its intellectual and monetary resources. Libraries have been experimenting in a variety of shared resource programs as a means of making quality more affordable, yet another application of the recurring theme that "tough times and rising costs have taught librarians at many colleges across the country that there is strength in numbers" (Carlson 2003, A30). Our consortial experience is just one of many that is taking place across the country.

Since the project fulfilled the consortium's stated mission, the next step was to determine whether or not each of the individual schools felt the addition of digital delivery of archival information was a viable possibility.

Though each of the libraries was willing to take a step in the digital direction, none were monetarily prepared to fully fund an individual effort. Purchasing the license as a group afforded the opportunity to "start small" and illustrates an important advantage of consortia. Not only are costs divided, but the learning process is facilitated. Had one individual from the smallest school actually found the money to move ahead, their learning process would have been in isolation, as most of the institutions are single person "shops." With seven participating institutions, however, there are more people with whom to collaborate and learn. There are more experiences from which to cull DAMS wisdom. As a consortium, these libraries and their responsible staff were able to make efficient headway on this initiative. In fact, these libraries exhibited a characteristic of a "visionary company"; they willingly stepped into a challenging situation and learned "by experimentation, trial and error, opportunism, and—quite literally—accident" (Collins 2001, 9). While they acted together collaboratively, it still benefits each of their programs!

DOES EXTERNAL DEMAND TRULY PLAY A MAJOR ROLE?

The initial meetings of key representatives from each of the schools revolved around institutional buy-in and whether or not there were collections that, once digitized, would fill a user need. As a representative of interested parties, the DIG met to discuss the digital landscape and began exploring whether or not there was an internal need to pursue the purchase of a DAMS. As stated previously, CLIC highly values the customer, and it aims to provide "improved and more comprehensive library resources and services to library users through the enhanced sharing of materials." Digital services are often cited as a way of improving customer satisfaction, and since each library serves a population that is increasingly digitally focused, a DAMS seemed a viable growth option that would fulfill this goal.

IMPROVING SERVICE

Not only would this digital endeavor better serve the external customer, thereby allowing researchers to access valuable historical documents without undue travel expenses, many schools believed that they could use the DAMS to facilitate intracampus use of archival photos by the alumni office or the marketing and communications department. It was agreed that expanding digital access was a logical extension of each of the library's archives. Additionally, there was a perceived demand by both the campus community and visiting researchers for a seamless search and retrieval process. Therefore, in the initial exploration phase, the DAMS was seen as a means of facilitating access to these unique collections while pursuing the consortium-wide goals such as improved and comprehensive resources, expanded content, and staff collegiality and training. Many of these initial assumptions about use have proved correct. One campus has set up a high use collection of college images that their marketing department uses on a regular basis. Northwestern College is concentrating on the digitization of its special collection, consisting of the sermons and papers of the school's founder, a prominent evangelical fundamentalist of the early 1900's, which is now being used on a regular basis by visiting researchers and students because of its Web presence and easy access! All of these successes are celebrated by the individual institutions and the consortial participants. Once it was established that there *were* underused resources and that there *was value* in implementing a digital delivery of those items, the committee embarked on the task of choosing a system.

SHARING THE COST

The reality of the situation is that this new initiative required a reallocation of library funds and employee responsibilities. While shifting funds in a time of financial hardship can be difficult and appear fool-hardy, a brief look at literature concerning the funding of academic libraries in particular does note that there continues to be a shift of resources to digital content and programing. As summarized in *2010 Top Ten Trends in Academic Libraries*, "digitization of unique library collections will increase and require a larger share of resources . . . because of the staffing, equipment, and storage costs associated with digital projects, libraries often must reallocate fiscal resources to support these functions" (ACRL 2010, 286). Even in light of this reallocation, the consortial agreement has allowed the participating institutions to bear less of the burden and feel fewer pains in the purchase, implementation, and upkeep process.

The committee investigated four DAMS over the course of several months. Each product exploration included a demonstration attended by all interested parties as well as a discussion meant to process the information shared and to explore the viability of each unique software suite. Members of the initial interest group, the DIG, directors of each library, and a collection of catalogers and information technology specialists attended each presentation. Presentations were planned at least two weeks in advance to insure that individuals had the opportunity to plan for the events.

Prior to the start of the presentations, the DIG felt that it would be useful to have a set of criteria available by which the schools could gauge the usefulness of each of the DAMS. It was very important to establish these discussion points to facilitate the group's eventual decision. This framework made clear any assumptions the participating institutions had about the future DAMS system and prevented any one school from claiming their needs had not received due consideration. The group's priorities required that the DAMS be

- usable by a consortium, with each school possessing the ability to create a branded user interface while at the same time using the same software. In other words, it was of the utmost importance that the DAMS allow for the autonomy of each individual library.
- Open Archives Initiative compliant.
- easy to implement and use "out of the box" but customizable.
- easily integrated with the catalog and with course management software.
- able to distribute high resolution images.
- able to distribute audio and video.
- able to handle robust metadata.
- able to utilize Optical Character Recognition software.
- fully searchable.
- self-archiving.

It is also important to note that each school representative realized there was no "one-stop" solution to their asset management needs. Coming into the agreement with a reasonable expectation prevented any undue disappointment.

In addition to establishing a clear set of criteria, the DIG also appointed a chairperson for the committee who would be responsible for facilitating communication with the CLIC Board. The chairperson worked closely with the CLIC executive director, the individual with whom each of the DAMS providers communicated.

Once the DIG identified a preferred DAMS, they were able to discuss the monetary responsibilities of each institution. Since the purpose of the joint purchase was to extend the buying power of each institution, it should be noted that as the projects evolve and the needs change, the financial agreement has been revisited. The parameters of the current agreement are as follows:

- Yearly product charges are shared equally among participating schools since each institution has equal access to the DAMS software and customer service.
- Yearly hosting fees are assigned based on each school's storage space use.

Discussion of costs included not only the hosting charges and the yearly fees associated with software but also the purchase of digitization equipment such as scanners and high quality cameras. After this discussion, it was decided that each school would be responsible for purchasing its own equipment. The group did, however, spend time brainstorming ways in which each school could make a wise decision about its purchases. These shared suggestions included the following:

- Collaboration with the institution's IT department
- Consulting the DAMS listserv as well as archive's listservs
- Familiarizing oneself with professional digitization standards and suggestions
- Reading technology reviews
- Talking with one another about our choices.

No one felt overwhelmed or uninformed about their purchases because each of us had the opportunity to share with one another what we learned in this exploratory phase, another advantage of the consortial endeavor.

Once these and similar decisions were made, members drafted a proposal that was submitted to the board for its approval. Researching the DAMS created a well-supported argument for the purchase of the system, and outlining the purchase agreement and participating institutional contribution was only the beginning of the hard work that has made this a successful endeavor.

POSTPURCHASE: SHARING THE BENEFITS

Once the involved parties agreed that (1) a DAMS would greatly improve the collection, organization, and dissemination of information to both internal and external library users; and (2) that the pursuit of this goal was most cost-effective when shared by the group it came time to purchase and implement the system. After reviewing the past three years of DIG meeting minutes, it would only be honest to say that this project has required patience, intentionality from all interested parties, a bit of creativity, and hard work.

The first order of business was to change the committee from an ad hoc interest group into a Digitization Operational Committee (DOC). As an operational group, the digitization committee now has a permanent status within CLIC and requires representation from each participating institution. Next, the newly formed operational committee needed to create a statement of purpose to help guide future decisions. After much thought, the DOC decided that each of the eight CLIC institutions will independently develop collections by selecting materials and adding content according to their institutional needs and resources. The goal is to produce and provide access to collections that add value, support teaching, learning, and scholarly research, and highlight unique collections held by the school. There was also the intentional acknowledgement of a possibility for future joint CLIC collections if a need arises and a viable opportunity presents itself. Lastly, it is clearly understood by those involved that the goal of collection development is to provide unrestricted access to materials that are free of copyright and legal restrictions. Although some collections have since been created that are restricted due to copyright and/or license stipulations, this aim remains consistent.

After laying out this framework, the group created a shared home page for the collections that included information about the consortium and this digital endeavor, the goals of the Digitization Operational Committee, and the mission of the DOC, which is "to provide an opportunity for cross functional collaboration and cooperation within CLIC's libraries, campuses, and perhaps outside the CLIC community. In doing so, the CLIC Digitization Operational Committee embraces the entrepreneurial spirit, institutional involvement, and awareness level of creating, maintaining, cataloging, and purchasing digital equipment and projects throughout CLIC institutions," and a list of contacts for each school.

In order to prevent future difficulties and to assure that each of the institutions felt they were integral to the success of the endeavor, the DOC made sure that everyone involved was clear about the following:

- The freedom to create within the general framework of the chosen identity schema
- Institutional responsibility for the creation of collections and appropriate metadata
- Frequency and necessity of DOC meeting (once a month for 1.5 hours)
- Well-organized avenues of communication, including goals, policies, procedures, wiki and a shared Website, and the importance of utilizing them

CREATING THE USER EXPERIENCE

An important concern was the system's customizability. Each of the institutions wanted to benefit from the shared costs while at the same time have the freedom to create a uniquely branded interface. In other words, it was of the utmost importance that the DAMS allow for the autonomy of each individual library. At the same time, all of the institutions agreed that to benefit users who may move between all of the collections, there should be a consistent feel among the collections and a similar navigational schema.

The first step in achieving this fine balance involved establishing a naming convention. Since all of the schools would be working in the same "back end" of the system, it was important that they have an agreed upon format for naming. The DOC defined their naming convention as follows: "[School Name] Name of the collection." Other style regulations included

- Each school's name should appear in the collection banner.
- Each school's colors would provide the framework for the color schema of its page.

As an added advantage to the consortial purchasing schema, CLIC paid for part-time internal tech support that would be available for several hours each week to all participating institutions to help design and format individual collection pages. This has had the advantage of

- helping schools with small staff move ahead on their projects
- insuring for the uniform appearance of each of the school's collection pages

We should point out, however, that the consortium carries the cost involved in this service.

INSTITUTIONAL RESPONSIBILITY

Each institution is responsible for the growth of its collections. However, there is an open and encouraging dialogue among institutions as they grow their collections. Not only are the types of items collected discussed, but the DOG also discusses acquisitions policies and procedures so that all representatives grow in their understanding of processes and refine their own practices—an example of staff collegiality and training that benefits everyone involved.

In addition to sharing acquisition work flows, the committee also created a project workflow to help guide, not dictate, the processes at each of the institutions. Combining the group's knowledge pool, everyone was able to build on one another's experience, training, and reading to efficiently and thoroughly outline helpful project management schemata. This is yet another example of how consortial collegiality can increase an individual institution's efficiency and distribution of professional development funds.

Another hot topic in the early stages of development was metadata conventions. As noted by McCord, "metadata flexibility is another requirement of the DAMS environment. Each discipline, school, project, or application type may require metadata structures—taxonomies are meaningful within the discipline or within the context of a work flow" (2002, 2). Realizing this, the DOC decided to allow each institution the opportunity to create its own metadata conventions. Members of the DOC have recently noted, however, that users may benefit from metadata collaboration. Common metadata added to individual collections may make it easier for users to search and discover across institutional collections, especially in instances of complimentary collections. Metadata is especially important because it is one of the primary features that add much more value to the institution and the information objects it creates.

COLLABORATION: ENHANCED REPUTATION

Once instituted, CONTENTdm allowed for collaboration between campus entities that was previously not possible. At several member institutions, the library became a major player in campus conversations about the use and management of digital assets. For example, Bethel has a Digital Library Advisory Committee that includes members from the offices of communications and marketing, parent and alumni services, Web services, libraries, and archives. This combination of relationships led to the funding and successful creation of the student newspaper collection and served as a launching pad for future projects. Since the newspaper collection's roll-out, others on campus have approached Bethel's digital librarian to express their excitement about participating in these digital initiatives as future collaborators. As these collections grow and find uses in and out of the classroom, other campus members begin to witness these services and realize how digital delivery of their department's content could highlight strengths and/or facilitate work. What follows, then, is a growing understanding of how the library can utilize valuable tools for the betterment of the educational community.

COMMUNICATION

One of the most valuable structures in place is the DOC's monthly meetings. In these meetings, all DAMS administrators, as well as additional interested parties, meet to discuss the current system, issues, advancements, current projects, and future project considerations. These monthly meetings, while not always groundbreaking, emphasize the shared nature of the product and foster a sense of collegiality and common purpose that facilitates cross-institutional communication.

It is also important that the involved institutions have a time and place to communicate concerning the collection distribution. The license purchased from OCLC limits the number of collections that can be created with the software. Since each school wanted to create collections uniquely geared toward its population's needs, it was necessary early on to determine the number of collections each institution had at its disposal. Much like the continued need to discuss cost distribution and responsibility, it is necessary to the success of the program that the institutions share information about collection size and development so that plans can be made to ensure that CONTENTdm continues to meet the consortium's needs. As in any case of program implementation in a consortial setting, some institutions will have greater monetary, staff, and time resources that will allow growth quicker than the programs that began the project as a way of pursuing a cost-effective, user-oriented program with the burgeoning digital service landscape in mind.

WHAT LIES AHEAD?

Collection management, or selecting the types of objects to collect, will play an important role in shaping the future direction of this project. While most schools started with unique and archival collections, there is a variety of new initiatives that could enhance and diversify the offerings of the current collection. For one, the current collections of participating institutions are distinctly research oriented, primary source, and or archival. This is not to say, however, that both students and faculty might not benefit from a records management arm of their digital initiative.

Another line of conversation worth pursuing would be the value and viability of beginning to collectively build a shared collection, pooling their time, resources, and funds to build additional collections. There are several collections, including the Minnesota Digital Library (MDL), that would model this type of collective collecting and inform future programs. Additionally, the availability and use of collections is another topic worth revisiting on a regular basis. Currently, collections are made available through the institution's catalog and Webpages as well as harvested in WorldCat. Google searches will often bring collections of interest to the attention of searchers at large.

Another topic for future discussion is whether or not DOC members may want to use MDL and its commerce-based services of photo reproduction, for example, as a revenue-making service. Research services for a fee may also naturally flow from greater exposure to an institution's special or unique collections.

Lastly, as the participating institutions cultivate new collaborations within their educational communities, it will be important to reassess goals and priorities. As the library institutions grow their collections and prove their usefulness within their communities, they will be able to reevaluate their services and mine other sources of monetary and intellectual support within their institutions. They will be able to conscientiously maintain strong relationships with early investors while growing new relationships to the benefit of their users.

ASSESSMENT AND REASSESSMENT

If anything should be taken away from this discussion, it is the fact that, while consortial relationships facilitate cost-effective growth strategies through the sharing of the monetary burden and the distribution of professional development and learning among a larger group of capable, service minded professionals, utilizing a DAMS is an endeavor that demands good communication, trust, and consistent reevaluation of costs and needs. Reevaluation assures that the model of cost-sharing remains beneficial to those in the agreement and also allows those involved the opportunity to collaborate and improve upon acquisitions, development, workflow and public relations. It should, however, be made clear that the consortium has not yet developed a set of evaluative points by which to clearly communicate with their institution's upper administration the value of this project.

In addition to revisiting the cost of the project, the DOC must also assess the value of the service. While some participants have used Google Analytics to track usage and others are actively using CONTENTdm's imbedded statistics tools, there is much room for improvement in this aspect of the project. That said, this project and its success must be considered through a lens of the program's value to the school, the consortium, and its community of users. The ultimate question should be, does this digitization program enrich the user experience while imparting value? We did not embark on this venture for the sake of using a tool and advertising our competence in the digital realm. Rather, we undertook this venture to improve our users' experience and make available valuable information in a more easily managed format.

REFERENCES

ACRL Research Planning and Review Committee. 2010. 2010 top ten trends in academic libraries. *College & Research Libraries News* 71:286–92.

American Library Association. 2007. Value of academic research libraries. http://www.ala.org/ala/mgrps/divs/acrl/issues/value/futures.cfm.

Branin, J. J. 2003. Institutional repositories. In *Encyclopedia of library and information science*, ed. Miriam Drake, 237–48. Boca Raton, FL: Taylor & Francis Group. https://kb.osu.edu/dspace/handle/1811/441.

Byrd, T. 2010. The Twenty-first century college library. Leaders look toward the future. http://www.neal-schuman.com/academic/Byrd2010.pdf.

Carlson, S. 2003. Libraries' consortium conundrum. *The Chronicle of Higher Education*, October 10, A30.

Carnegie Classifications Institution Lookup. 2010. Carnegie classifications. http://classifications.carnegiefoundation.org/lookup_listings/institution.php.

Collins, J. C. 2001. *Good to great: Why some companies make the leap . . . and others don't.* New York: HarperBusiness.

Dempsey, B. 2010. For love or money. *Library Journal.* 135(15). http://www.libraryjournal.com/lj/home/886465264/survey_on_fees_for_library.html.csp.

Dickeson, R. C. 2010. *Prioritizing academic programs and services: Reallocating resources to achieve strategic balance.* San Francisco: Jossey-Bass Publishers.

Khosrow-Pour, M. 2005. *Encyclopedia of information science and technology.* Hershey, PA: Idea Group Reference.

Lederman, D. 2010. News: The pressure to prioritize. *Inside Higher Ed*, November 11. http://www.insidehighered.com/news/2010/11/11/priorities.

Lynch, C. 2009. "Special collections at the cusp of the digital age: A credo." Association of Research Libraries. http://www.arl.org/bm˜doc/rli-267-lynch.pdf.

Markey, K., B. St. Jean, S. Y. Rieh, E. Yakel, and J. Kim. 2008. Institutional repositories: The experience of master's and baccalaureate institutions. *Portal: Libraries and the Academy* 8:157–73.

McCord, A. 2002. "Overview of digital asset management systems." EDUCAUSE Evolving Technologies Committee. http://net.educause.edu/ir/library/pdf/DEC0203.pdf.

Murray, J. 2010. Toward collaboration. Leaders look toward the future. http://www.neal-schuman.com/academic/murray2010.pdf

Nolan, C. W., and J. Costanza. 2006. Promoting and archiving student work through an institutional repository: Trinity university, LASR, and the digital commons. *Serials Review* 32:92–98.

Xia, J., and D. B. Opperman. 2010. Current trends in institutional repositories for institutions offering master's and baccalaureate degrees. *Serials Review* 36:10–18.

APPENDIX

School Characteristics Using the Carnegie System for Classifying Institutions of Higher Education

Augsburg College—Enrollment (2003–2004) 3,375; (Fall 2009) 4,054

Undergraduate Instructional Program:	Bal/SGC: Balanced arts & sciences/professions, some graduate coexistence
Graduate Instructional Program:	Postbac-A&S/Other: Postbaccalaureate with arts & sciences (other dominant fields)
Enrollment Profile:	HU: High undergraduate
Undergraduate Profile:	FT4/S/HTI: Full-time four-year, selective, higher transfer-in
Size and Setting:	S4/R: Small four-year, primarily residential
Basic:	Master's S: Master's Colleges and Universities (smaller programs)

Bethel University—Enrollment (2003–2004) 3,605; (Fall 2009) 6,400 (includes seminary ~1000)

Undergraduate Instructional Program:	Prof+A&S/SGC: Professions plus arts & sciences, some graduate coexistence
Graduate Instructional Program:	Postbac-A&S/Ed: Postbaccalaureate with arts & sciences (education dominant)
Enrollment Profile:	HU: High undergraduate
Undergraduate Profile:	FT4/MS/LTI: Full-time four-year, more selective, lower transfer-in
Size and Setting:	M4/HR: Medium four-year, highly residential
Basic:	Master's M: Master's Colleges and Universities (medium programs)

Concordia University–St. Paul—Enrollment (2003–2004) 2,217; (Fall 2009) 2,816

Undergraduate Instructional Program:	Prof-F/SGC: Professions focus, some graduate coexistence
Graduate Instructional Program:	Postbac-A&S/Bus: Postbaccalaureate with arts & sciences (business dominant)
Enrollment Profile:	HU: High undergraduate
Undergraduate Profile:	FT4/S/HTI: Full-time four-year, selective, higher transfer-in
Size and Setting:	S4/NR: Small four-year, primarily nonresidential
Basic:	Master's M: Master's Colleges and Universities (medium programs)

Hamline University—Enrollment (2003–2004) 4,022; (Fall 2009) 4,800

Undergraduate Instructional Program:	A&S+Prof/SGC: Arts & sciences plus professions, some graduate coexistence
Graduate Instructional Program:	S-Doc/Ed: Single doctoral (education)
Enrollment Profile:	MU: Majority undergraduate
Undergraduate Profile:	FT4/S/HTI: Full-time four-year, selective, higher transfer-in
Size and Setting:	M4/R: Medium four-year, primarily residential
Basic:	Master's L: Master's Colleges and Universities (larger programs)

Notes:

- Graduate degree program classification is based on fewer than 50 degrees.
- Graduate program classification is based on fewer than 10 doctoral degrees, and this institution awarded 100 or more master's or professional degrees.

Macalester College—Enrollment (2003–2004) 1,900; (Fall 2009) 1996

Undergraduate Instructional Program:	A&S-F/NGC: Arts & sciences focus, no graduate coexistence
Graduate Instructional Program:	(not applicable)
Enrollment Profile:	ExU4: Exclusively undergraduate four-year
Undergraduate Profile:	FT4/MS/LTI: Full-time four-year, more selective, lower transfer-in
Size and Setting:	S4/HR: Small four-year, highly residential
Basic:	Bac/A&S: Baccalaureate Colleges–Arts & Sciences

Northwestern College—Enrollment (2003–2004) 2,734; (Fall 2009) 3,070

Undergraduate Instructional Program:	Prof+A&S/NGC: Professions plus arts & sciences, no graduate coexistence
Graduate Instructional Program:	(not applicable)
Enrollment Profile:	ExU4: Exclusively undergraduate four-year
Undergraduate Profile:	FT4/S/HTI: Full-time four-year, selective, higher transfer-in
Size and Setting:	S4/R: Small four-year, primarily residential
Basic:	Bac/Diverse: Baccalaureate Colleges–Diverse Fields

St. Catherine University—Enrollment (2003–2004) 4,809; (Fall 2009) 5,277

Undergraduate Instructional Program:	Bal/SGC: Balanced arts & sciences/professions, some graduate coexistence
Graduate Instructional Program:	Postbac-A&S/Ed: Postbaccalaureate with arts & sciences (education dominant)
Enrollment Profile:	HU: High undergraduate
Undergraduate Profile:	MFT4/S/HTI: Medium full-time four-year, selective, higher transfer-in
Size and Setting:	M4/R: Medium four-year, primarily residential
Basic:	Master's L: Master's Colleges and Universities (larger programs)

University of Saint Thomas—Enrollment (2003–2004) 10,474; (Fall 2010) 10,839

Undergraduate Instructional Program:	Bal/SGC: Balanced arts & sciences/professions, some graduate coexistence
Graduate Instructional Program:	Doc/Prof: Doctoral, professions dominant
Enrollment Profile:	MU: Majority undergraduate
Undergraduate Profile:	FT4/MS/LTI: Full-time four-year, more selective, lower transfer-in
Size and Setting:	M4/R: Medium four-year, primarily residential
Basic:	DRU: Doctoral/Research Universities

Index

Page numbers in *Italics* represent tables.
Page numbers in **Bold** represent figures.